W9-AWC-322

Lent, Holy Week, Easter,
and the Great Fifty Days

Lent, Holy Week, Easter, and the Great Fifty Days

A Ceremonial Guide

Leonel L. Mitchell

COWLEY PUBLICATIONS
Cambridge ✦ Boston
Massachusetts

© 1996 by Leonel L. Mitchell
All rights reserved.

Published in the United States of America by Cowley Publications, a division of the Society of St. John the Evangelist. No portion of this book may be reproduced, stored in or introduced into a retrieval system, or transmitted, in any form or by any means—including photocopying—without the prior written permission of Cowley Publications, except in the case of brief quotations embodied in critical articles and reviews.

Library of Congress Cataloging-in-Publication Data:
Mitchell, Leonel L. (Leonel Lake), 1930–
    Lent, Holy Week, Easter, and the great fifty days : a ceremonial guide / Leonel L. Mitchell.
        p.   cm.
    "This volume is a companion to The ceremonies of the Eucharist: a guide to celebration by the late Howard E. Galley"—Pref.
    Includes bibliographical references.
    ISBN: 1-56101-134-7 (alk. paper)
    1. Lent. 2. Easter. 3. Holy Week services. 4. Easter service. 5. Episcopal Church—Liturgy.
    I. Galley, Howard. Ceremonies of the Eucharist. II. Title.
    BV85.M57 1996
    264'.03—dc20   96-24910
                                                                    CIP

Scripture quotations are from the *New Revised Standard Version* of the Bible, © 1989 by the Division of Christian Education of the National Council of the Churches of Christ in the USA. Used by permission. All rights reserved.

Editors: Cynthia Shattuck and Vicki Black
Designer: Vicki Black

This book is printed on recycled, acid-free paper and was produced in the United States of America.

Cowley Publications
28 Temple Place
Boston, Massachusetts 02111

In memory of Howard E. Galley

Cross references in this book refer to chapter sections and subsections, as listed in the Table of Contents. Thus 1.2 refers to the section The Service in Detail in the chapter on Ash Wednesday, and 1.2a refers to the subsection The Procession within that section.

The following abbreviations are used for these liturgical books referenced throughout this book. Page numbers refer to these editions unless otherwise noted.

BCP   *The Book of Common Prayer* (1979)

BOS   *The Book of Occasional Services* (1994)

LFF   *Lesser Feasts and Fasts* (1994)

LHWE   *Lent, Holy Week, Easter* (1986)

BAS   *The Book of Alternative Services* (1985)

Contents

EASTER AND THE GREAT FIFTY DAYS

Preface

This volume is a companion to *The Ceremonies of the Eucharist: A Guide to Celebration* by the late Howard E. Galley.[1] The general descriptions of the church and its furnishings, the liturgical ministries, music and liturgical practices, and the detailed directions for celebrating the eucharist and baptism given in *The Ceremonies of the Eucharist* are assumed in this volume and will not be repeated. Specifically, this guide to the liturgies of Lent, Holy Week, Easter, and the Great Fifty Days is intended for "all who bear responsibility for the planning and conduct of public worship" in medium-sized Episcopal churches. There are, in addition, directions for celebrating the major Holy Week liturgies in small congregations with fewer liturgical resources. Some congregations will find themselves in between the two descriptions, and will wish to follow the more elaborate model for some things and the simpler version for others. Other congregations will have even more resources available—two or more deacons, a number of priests, a large choir.

---

1. Cambridge, Mass.: Cowley Publications, 1989.

It needs to be said of books of ceremonial in general, and of this one in particular, that they often seem much more directive than they intend to be. Descriptions of services appear as a series of imperatives which, in the minds of some, attain a certain prescriptive value. But this is not really the case. The rubrics are directions for the celebration of the rites of *The Book of Common Prayer* or other service book. They are not intended to be straightjackets in which to bind the liturgical assembly. Obviously, some rubrics contain theologically significant statements about how the rite must be conducted to conform to the tradition of the Episcopal Church, or even of the Christian religion. Others set out a coherent way in which to accomplish this, and may require adapting to local conditions: directions which imply a church of a certain shape and arrangement and must be adapted to buildings of other shapes are an obvious example. Ceremonial guides are intended to interpret all of this in the light of a set of traditional (or nontraditional) liturgical principles.

The directions in this book provide a reasonable, consistent way in which to celebrate these liturgies. It is by no means the only possible way. The liturgy grows out of the life of actual individual congregations, and no two congregations will celebrate the liturgy in exactly the same way. Congregations are often extremely creative in their adaptation of the official liturgies to their particular circumstances. This is to be encouraged as long as it is consonant with the spirit of the celebration, but it is often impossible to export this creativity from one congregation to another.

The Episcopal Church is not a monocultural, English-speaking church. Its worship is conducted in many languages by people of many cultures, and these differences can and should affect the way in which liturgies are celebrated. These rites are celebrated in Spanish, French, Korean, and several Native American languages, among others, and the linguistic groups and the cultures which use them will all approach the liturgy in different ways, using different cultural idioms. Hispanic Holy Week customs and the all-night vigil traditions of the Lakotas readily find their place in the liturgical celebrations, but it would be a mistake for someone of a different culture, such as this writer, to attempt to tell them how to adapt the liturgies to their needs.

It is my intention in describing these liturgies to include everything that may reasonably be done, assuming that it is easier for a congregation to omit things that are described than to wonder how to do things that have been omitted.

I wish to acknowledge gratefully the assistance of the Rev. Jeffrey Lee and Deacon Ormonde Plater, who read the manuscript and made many helpful suggestions.

It was Howard Galley's intention to complete his earlier work with a second volume dealing with Lent, Holy Week, and Easter, and another with the pastoral offices. This volume on the paschal cycle is an earnest on his intention, and is dedicated to his memory. The ideas and implementation, however, are mine, and should not be blamed on Howard.

The Paschal Cycle

The paschal mystery of the dying and rising again of Jesus Christ and our participation therein is the theological core of the gospel, and its liturgical celebration is the central event of the church year. This celebration includes not only the special services of Holy Week and the Easter Vigil, but a substantial part of the year, roughly from February to June, the seasons of Lent, Holy Week, and Easter.

Not only is celebration of the resurrection of Christ theologically central to this annual cycle, the entire celebration of the paschal cycle is "dependent upon the movable date of the Sunday of the Resurrection or Easter Day" (BCP 15). Easter is actually a fixed date in a lunar calendar. Its earliest recorded celebration was among the Quartodecimans of Asia Minor, who celebrated the *Pascha* on the fourteenth day of the Jewish month of Nisan. Irenaeus claimed that this celebration went back to the time of Polycarp, who died around 155. It celebrated both the passion and resurrection of

Christ. In other parts of the Christian world, and eventually everywhere, the celebration was held on the Sunday following, Sunday being the weekly eschatological celebration of the resurrection. In our calendar Easter Day is the Sunday after the first full moon of spring. It therefore falls between March 22 and April 25.

The celebration of the *Pascha* included both fasting and celebration. In the Roman model, which became normative, Friday and Saturday were observed as days of fasting, with the celebration of the eucharist either during Saturday night or at dawn on Sunday, so that it occurred on the first day of the week (which began at sundown in the Jewish world but at midnight in the Roman). The festival rejoicing continued for fifty days, called the Pentecost, all of which were treated as one great Lord's Day, celebrating the resurrection and ascension of Jesus and the descent of the Holy Spirit.

In the fourth century the week before Easter came to be filled with celebrations tied to the historical commemoration of the resurrection on Sunday. The Friday, already a fast day, became Good Friday, the commemoration of the passion and crucifixion; the Last Supper "on the night in which he was betrayed" was commemorated with a Thursday evening eucharist. From this grows our Holy Week. At about the same time the period of preparation of catechumens for Easter baptism, marked by penitence, fasting, and instruction, came to be identified as *Quadragesima* (the Forty Days), which we translate as Lent.

The Easter cycle of the liturgical year in our Prayer Book developed from the medieval version of this sequence of celebrations. The Proper Liturgies for Special Days mark major occasions in this cycle. As we observe these separate occasions, though, we need to keep in mind the unity of the entire celebration. The Great Vigil of Easter, with the celebration of the paschal sacraments of baptism and eucharist, is at its core and is its organizing theme, but the Easter cycle encompasses everything from Ash Wednesday through Pentecost. Its theme is the salvation of the human race through the mighty acts of Jesus Christ. In its celebration we become participants in those mighty acts and enter into the risen life of Christ.

LENT

Chapter One

Ash Wednesday

Although Lent has always been described as forty days in length, there actually has been no agreement as to how the days were to be counted. In the Western church Lent usually began on *Quadragesima* Sunday, our First Sunday in Lent, as it still does in the Ambrosian rite of Milan. This is exactly forty days before Good Friday, the beginning of the older paschal fast. The fast began the Monday following. The so-called season of Pre-Lent represents attempts to begin Lent earlier, counting the days in various ways. In the sixth century the beginning of the fast was moved to the Wednesday before Lent 1, in order to provide forty fast days before Easter. This is our Ash Wednesday, which then became the first day of Lent.

The ceremony from which its popular name is taken has its roots in the Old Testament, where covering oneself with sackcloth and ashes was a sign of repentance and mourning. Early Christians also used sackcloth and ashes as a sign of their repentance. In eighth-century Rome an antiphon was sung during the opening procession on the first day of Lent which mentioned putting on sackcloth and ashes. The Romans interpreted it spiritually, but in Northern Europe the actual imposition of ashes was begun in order to give liturgical expression to the text. In 1091 a North Italian council ordered everyone to receive ashes "on Ash Wednesday."

Another significant, and older, rite on that day was the admission of public penitents to their penitential discipline, so that they might be readmitted to communion before Easter. With the end of public penance, penitential exercises were adopted by the entire congregation during the Lenten season. This gave to Ash Wednesday its character as a Christian *yom kippur,* a day of atonement, of fasting and penitence for sin.

In *The Book of Common Prayer* penitence and fasting are the Ash Wednesday themes; the Litany of Penitence, with its solemn absolution at its close, is a liturgical expression of these themes. The (optional) imposition of ashes, as in its original introduction, is intended to give them ceremonial embodiment. Taken together these proper rites remind us that we stand before God as sinners doomed to die, and that it is only through God's merciful gift that we can hope for anything else. These are *Ash Wednesday* themes, however; they are not the only *Lenten* themes, and we make a mistake if we try to make the whole of Lent one long Ash Wednesday. The meaning not only of the imposition of ashes but of the day itself is expressed both in the prayer said by the presider before the imposition of ashes and by the words used during it: "Remember that you are dust, and to dust you shall return" (BCP 265). The prayer said over the ashes asks:

> Almighty God, you have created us out of the dust of the earth: Grant that these ashes may be to us a sign of our mortality and penitence, that we may remember that it is only by your gracious gift that we are given everlasting life.... (BCP 265)

The Book of Occasional Services, as a part of its Preparation of Baptized Persons for Reaffirmation of the Baptismal Covenant, contains a rite entitled Enrollment for Lenten Preparation. In editions prior to 1994 it was named The Calling of the Baptized to Continual Conversion. It is to be celebrated at the principal service on Ash Wednesday.

> In [this rite], baptized persons who have been exploring the implications of their baptismal covenant and are preparing to reaffirm it

at the coming Easter Vigil are recognized as examples of conversion for the congregation in its journey towards Easter. (BOS 141-142)

The rite itself takes place following the Blessing of the Ashes and before their imposition. In it the baptized persons are presented to the presider,[1] who questions their sponsors about the candidates' commitment and participation, gives a blessing to the persons presented, and imposes ashes upon them. The candidates assist the presider in imposing ashes upon the congregation. This rite is part of a contemporary adaptation of the catechumenate for use with those already baptized and is parallel to the admission of catechumens as candidates for baptism on the First Sunday in Lent. The rite itself borrows elements from the penitential rite mentioned above. Its central meaning is expressed in the presider's prayer of blessing:

Renew your Holy Spirit in them that they may lead us in our turning back to you as they prepare to celebrate with us Christ's passage from death to life.... (BOS 143)

If the parish is preparing baptized persons for the formal reaffirmation of their baptismal covenant at the Great Vigil, the rite is included in the principal Ash Wednesday celebration.

1. Preparations for the Service

The ashes, if they are to be used, need to be prepared beforehand. This is often more difficult in practice than in theory. They are traditionally made by burning the palms from the previous Palm Sunday. This should be done outdoors, with suitable precautions. Once they are burned the coarser

---

1. *The Book of Common Prayer* regularly refers to the presiding priest at the eucharist as the celebrant. Mindful that all of the participants are equally celebrants of the liturgy, I have preferred the term presider, except when quoting the Prayer Book.

pieces must be strained out and the residue reduced to powder. A strainer and a mortar and pestle, or any of the kitchen implements used to grind food, will work well. The ashes should be placed in one or more appropriate containers (one for each person distributing ashes). The containers should be small enough to hold in one hand, so that the thumb of the right hand may be used to sign a cross on the foreheads of the recipients. They are placed on the credence table, or in some other convenient place where they may easily be brought to the presider for the prayer over the ashes. A small table on which to place the ashes for the blessing may be needed.

If the Enrollment for Lenten Preparation (from *The Book of Occasional Services*) is to be used, and it is desired to have the persons presented kneel, appropriate kneeling cushions or benches will be needed. Considering the difficulty many people have in kneeling without a support to help them rise, it may be preferable to have them remain standing and bow their heads, unless they are to kneel at the communion rail.

The church should be decorated for Lent (see below) and Lenten vestments should be worn. The Prayer Book expects the principal service of Ash Wednesday to be a eucharist. Although it raises the possibility that it will be simply a liturgy of the Word, few congregations who have a priest available to preside at the eucharist will wish to avail themselves of that option.[2] Since it is a working day, the main celebration will probably be in the evening, so that most people can attend. Churches in the "downtown business district" may, of course, wish to schedule their principal liturgy for noon. The important consideration is not the hour but making it possible for the greatest number to participate. There may well be other services, and all may be celebrations of the eucharist with the proper Ash Wednesday features. (The directions for doing the liturgy in a small parish may be useful for the other celebrations.)

---

2. This option is discussed below in section 1.5, Ash Wednesday without a Priest.

2. The Service in Detail

a. The Procession

There is no entrance rite on Ash Wednesday. The liturgy begins with the salutation ("The Lord be with you") and the collect of the day. The procession may enter in silence, or a penitential hymn or psalm may be sung. Silent entry, as is rubrically required on Good Friday, places the day in marked contrast to the "normal" Sunday liturgy and associates it with Good Friday, the other major fast day.

The procession should be in the usual order. The deacon may carry the gospel book and place it on the altar. If there is more than one deacon in the congregation, they divide the diaconal duties. When not otherwise occupied deacons take their places on either side of the presiding priest or bishop. The priest goes directly to the chair after reverencing the altar and, when everyone is in place, sings (or says) "The Lord be with you" and the Ash Wednesday collect. If the chair is not conveniently placed it may be necessary to say the collect from the center of the sanctuary, facing the people. The acolyte holds the book open to the proper place. The readings and sermon follow in the usual manner.

b. The Invitation to a Holy Lent

The preacher may appropriately read the invitation to the observance of a holy Lent from the pulpit or other place of preaching at the conclusion of the sermon. Alternatively, it may be read by the presider, standing in the center of the sanctuary facing the people. At its conclusion all kneel. The presider and deacon kneel on the lowest step facing the altar, or other convenient place where they can visibly lead the congregation in silent prayer. A preacher leaves the pulpit to kneel. Others in the sanctuary should kneel in place, facing the altar. In some church buildings a focus other than the altar, such as a cross or icon, may be the appropriate center of prayerful attention. There is sign value in the leaders of worship kneeling on this occasion, but if they are unable to kneel, they may, or course, bow. They remain kneeling in silence long enough for people to think about repentance and mortality and to become uncomfortable.

The containers of ashes are placed on a small table brought by the acolyte to the center of the sanctuary. If there will be only two or three containers of ashes, the servers may hold them while the priest says the prayer over the ashes. The presider says the prayer facing the people with hand extended over the ashes. If desired, the ashes may be sprinkled with holy water and censed by the priest after the blessing.

c. Enrollment for Lenten Preparation

If the Enrollment for Lenten Preparation is to take place, the senior warden or other representative of the congregation brings the candidates forward and presents them. The presider and deacon face the candidates and presenter. It would be proper for the candidates and presenter to stand at the bottom of the chancel or sanctuary step facing the altar, with their sponsors standing behind them and the presider, deacon, and acolyte (holding *The Book of Occasional Services*) facing the congregation. It would be better for the candidates and ministers to face each other choirwise across the chancel, so that the congregation might see the faces of the candidates. Usually the ministers stand at the liturgical south, but the architecture of a particular church might suggest they stand on the other side, or in a different configuration. The purpose is for all to be visible to the congregation.

The presenter makes the presentation of the candidates all together, using their Christian names. The presider addresses the sponsors, who respond. The candidates kneel or bow their heads, in a row, with their sponsors behind them. The sponsors place a hand on their shoulders. The priest reads the blessing with both hands extended over the candidates, palms down, the acolyte holding the book.

The candidates stand if they are kneeling, and the presider says to them, "Receive ashes as a symbol of repentance and conversion and show us by your example how to turn to Christ" (BOS 143). The imposition of ashes then follows.

d. The Imposition of Ashes

The deacon imposes ashes on the presider, who remains in place. The presider then imposes ashes on the candidates (if the Enrollment for Lenten Preparation has been celebrated), the deacon, and the other ministers. This is most easily done if the presider stands in a central location in front of the altar and those in the sanctuary come forward to receive the ashes.

Ashes are administered by placing the right thumb in the ashes, marking a small cross on the person's forehead, and saying, "Remember that you are dust, and to dust you shall return" (BCP 265). The recipients may stand or kneel. Enough people should be used to impose ashes to make the ceremony move quickly. Imposition is not restricted to the clergy, although the presider and deacon should be included. The Enrollment for Lenten Preparation expects that the baptized candidates will assist in imposing ashes. They should do so wearing their street clothes.

The most expedient way to impose ashes on a large congregation is to set up stations at various places in the church and have the congregation come to those stations and receive the ashes standing. It may be pastorally easier to have the people receive ashes in the same manner in which they are accustomed to receive communion. It will be necessary either to announce how this is to be done, or to print an announcement in the program, or both.

All who have imposed ashes will need to wash their hands. They go to the credence table or a place near it to do this. If there are many imposers, several basins may be used, acolytes pouring water over their hands. Each person requires a separate towel.

During the imposition of ashes Psalm 51:1-18 is sung. Settings of this psalm are in *The Plainsong Psalter* and *The Anglican Chant Psalter.* It may also be sung to a simplified Anglican chant from *The Hymnal 1982* or any other convenient setting. Note that only verses 1-18 are sung, and the *Gloria Patri* is omitted. At its conclusion all who are not already kneeling kneel. The priest and deacon return to their central place, kneeling on the lowest step of the altar. If the imposition of ashes is omitted, Psalm 51 is sung (or said) kneeling immediately after the silence.

e. The Litany of Penitence and Holy Communion

The presider begins the Litany of Penitence. At its conclusion, the priest stands and faces the people to say the absolution. The acolyte likewise stands, holding the book for the priest. The priest makes the sign of the cross over the congregation at "He pardons and absolves...."

The Nicene Creed is omitted and the Litany of Penitence replaces the Prayers of the People and Confession of Sin. The Peace is exchanged, and the liturgy continues from the offertory in the usual way. When the Enrollment for Lenten Preparation is used, the second Lenten preface is required.

The solemn Prayer over the People from *The Book of Occasional Services* (BOS 24-25) replaces the blessing at the conclusion of the liturgy. The deacon says, "Bow down before the Lord," the people kneel (according to the rubric in *The Book of Occasional Services*) or bow (as the deacon has bidden), and the presider says the prayer with hands extended over the people. The first of the prayers provided is used on Ash Wednesday.

3. Other Ash Wednesday Services

If Evensong is sung on Shrove Tuesday, it is the final service of the post-Epiphany season, not a part of Lent. The Alleluias are used, both at the opening versicles and at the dismissal, and the traditional office hymn, "Alleluia, song of gladness" (Hymn 122/123), made be sung. A banner bearing the word "Alleluia" may be displayed in the church during the service and carried out at its close. This farewell to Alleluia is often incorporated into the liturgy of the Last Sunday after Epiphany. The purpose of these customs is to underscore the suppression of Alleluia from Ash Wednesday until the Great Vigil.

If it is desired to have something other than the proper liturgy for one of the Ash Wednesday services, a good alternative would be Morning Prayer with a Lenten Opening Sentence, the Confession of Sin, no Alleluia, Psalm 95 in place of the *Venite*, *Kyrie pantokrator* (Canticle 14) and *Benedictus* (Canticle 16) as the canticles, and a homily after the second lesson. This should provide a robust penitential beginning for the day and the season.

4. Ash Wednesday in Small Congregations

The Ash Wednesday liturgy can be effectively celebrated quite simply. A lector to read the lessons before the gospel is normal. If music is available, Lenten hymns and simple service music may be used.

The presider, deacon, and acolyte enter in silence. The presider goes to the chair and says the salutation and the collect for the day. The acolyte may hold the book, or it may be placed on a stand at a height suitable for reading. The presider sits for the readings. If the gradual psalm is not sung it may be read, either responsively by the lector (or celebrant) and congregation, or in unison.

The presider reads the invitation to the observance of a holy Lent either from the pulpit, or from the sanctuary or chancel step. Everyone, including the presider, kneels. The presider kneels in the center of the sanctuary, on the lowest altar step (if there is one). They remain kneeling long enough to think about repentance and mortality and to become uncomfortable.

The presider stands, faces the people, and says the prayer over the ashes, if they are to be used. The acolyte may hold the container of ashes. It is desirable that some other person (priest, deacon, lector, eucharistic minister, or acolyte) impose ashes on the presider. If no such person is available, the presider marks a cross of ashes on his or her own forehead. The presider then imposes ashes on those in the sanctuary and the congregation. If the congregation is large enough, another person (priest, deacon, lector, lay eucharistic minister, or adult acolyte) may assist in the imposition. The congregation may come forward to a station (or stations) to receive the ashes, or they may come to the communion rail. Some announcement of the procedure will be necessary.

During the imposition, Psalm 51:1-18 may be sung by a cantor or choir, or it may be read. If it is to be read, it is best read by the congregation kneeling, after the imposition, immediately before the Litany of Penitence.

The presider leads the Litany of Penitence, kneeling in the center of the sanctuary before the altar. The priest stands and faces the congregation to give the absolution.

The Nicene Creed is omitted and the Litany of Penitence replaces the Prayers of the People and Confession of Sin. The Peace is exchanged, and the liturgy continues from the offertory in the usual way. The Lenten Prayer over the People (BOS 24-25) replaces the blessing. The deacon or presider says, "Bow down before the Lord." The people kneel, and the presider says the prayer with hands extended toward the congregation.

5. Ash Wednesday without a Priest

If the congregation has no priest, the proper liturgy of the day may be led by a deacon or lay person. A deacon may preside from the presidential chair, a deacon's chair, or the officiant's stall in choir. This would be a proper place for a lay presider, but in a small church building there may well be only one appropriate place from which to preside at a service. A deacon may wear an alb (or surplice) and stole, or an alb, dalmatic, and stole; a lay presider may wear a cassock and surplice, or an alb.

The entrance should be in silence and may include only the presider, or the presider and an acolyte. The presider faces the congregation and says, "The Lord be with you," and the Ash Wednesday collect. The presider sits and a lector reads the first two lessons. The presider should watch the lector, so as to focus the congregation's attention on the reading. If the gradual psalm is not sung, it may be read by the congregation in unison, or responsively with the presider.

If the presider is a deacon, the gospel may be read in the traditional manner. A lay presider goes to the lectern and reads the gospel as a lesson, or a lector does so. If the presider is not a preacher, an appropriate homily may be read. At the very least a portion of a patristic homily such as those provided for Ash Wednesday in Howard Galley's *The Prayer Book Office* or J. Robert Wright's *Readings for the Daily Office from the Early Church* can be read.

The presider or the lector reads the invitation to the observance of a holy Lent from the lectern. All kneel in silence long enough for everyone to think about repentance and mortality and to become uncomfortable. The presider stands to say the prayer over the ashes. Someone (lector, eucharistic minister, vestry member, or acolyte) goes to the presider and imposes ashes. The presider then imposes ashes on the congregation as described above. If the congregation is large enough someone else may assist in the imposition. After the imposition the imposers go to the credence table and wash their hands.

The presider kneels. Unless Psalm 51 has been read or sung during the imposition, it is read in unison by the congregation. The presider leads the Litany for Penitence. At its conclusion, the presider, still kneeling, reads the prayer for forgiveness from Morning Prayer (BCP 80), substituting "us" for "you" and "our" for "your." The service concludes with the exchange of the Peace.

It will almost always be desirable to follow the Prayer Book's general directions for services "if there is no Communion" by singing a hymn or anthem, taking up a collection and receiving the people's offerings, and concluding the service with the Lord's Prayer and the Grace (BCP 407).

Chapter Two

Lent

A sh Wednesday is the opening of the season of Lent. Lent is an Anglo-Saxon word for "spring" which is used to translate the Latin *Quadragesima*, Forty Days. Since the fourth century it has been described as a penitential season of forty days, corresponding to the final period of preparation for candidates for Easter baptism. The meaning of the season is well expressed is the invitation to the celebration of a holy Lent in *The Book of Common Prayer*:

> The first Christians observed with great devotion the days of our Lord's passion and resurrection, and it became the custom of the Church to prepare for them by a season of penitence and fasting. This season of Lent provided a time in which converts to the faith were prepared for Holy Baptism. It was also a time when those who, because of notorious sins, had been separated from the body of the faithful were reconciled by penitence and forgiveness, and restored to the fellowship of the Church. Thereby, the whole congregation was put in mind of the message of pardon and absolution set forth in the Gospel of our Savior, and of the need which all Christians continually have to renew their repentance and faith. (BCP 264-265)

Preparation of the candidates for baptism at the Great Vigil of Easter is the primary purpose of Lent, and if there will be catechumens preparing for Easter baptism, then the rites of their preparation need to take a principal place in Lenten planning. The enrollment of candidates for baptism at the Great Vigil takes place on the First Sunday in Lent. *The Book of Occasional Services* contains the form, as well as prayers and blessings which may be used before the Prayers of the People on the Third, Fourth, and Fifth Sundays in Lent. Both the candidates for baptism and their sponsors, and those baptized persons who are preparing to reaffirm their vows at the Great Vigil and have participated in the Enrollment for Lenten Preparation (the name given in the 1994 edition of *The Book of Occasional Services* to the rite formerly called Calling of the Baptized to Continuing Conversion) on Ash Wednesday are prayed for by name during the Prayers of the People during Lent. *The Book of Occasional Services* requires that the two groups be prayed for separately, that is, in separate petitions. The purpose of this requirement is to avoid confusing catechumens, who are unbaptized persons preparing for baptism, with those preparing to renew their vows. It is important that the rites recognize that those already baptized are Christians and members of the church.

In addition, the names of the candidates for baptism and their sponsors are properly mentioned in the intercessions of Eucharistic Prayer D, if that is used during Lent. *The Book of Occasional Services* describes candidacy for baptism as involving in addition to the rites "the private disciplines of fasting, examination of conscience, and prayer," and commends the ancient custom of the sponsors joining in the prayer and fasting (BOS 116).

Though the actual programs for the formation of the candidates are outside the scope of this volume, a brief word is in order. In fourth-century Jerusalem, the content of the catechesis was the Bible and the creed. A modern adaptation of the catechumenate, following the call of the 1988 General Convention for the implementation of an adult catechumenate and parallel rites for the baptized, is provided in *The Catechumenal Process: Adult Initiation and Formation for Christian Life and Ministry*.[1] Materials published for use with the Roman Catholic Rite for Christian

Initiation of Adults (RCIA) can also be adapted for use in the Episcopal Church. These materials are important whether or not the congregation has adult candidates for baptism in a particular year, because what is necessary for the formation of new members is generally what is also necessary for the renewal of old members: a program designed for cate-chumens will often be the same program needed for parish Lenten renewal. Recognition of this was a major factor in the extension of Lenten fasting and penitence from the catechumens and the sponsors to the entire congregation.

Lent is therefore a season of repentance and renewal for the entire congregation. The same Lenten exhortation urges self-examination, repentance, prayer, fasting, and self-denial, as well as reading and meditating on God's word as the means to the observance of a holy Lent (BCP 365). The second Lenten preface speaks of preparing "with joy" for the coming feast and adds works of mercy and renewal in word and sacrament to the appropriate means. The elements of joy and renewal are as important as prayer, fasting, and self-denial in the Lenten observance, which otherwise becomes a forty day repetition of Ash Wednesday.

1. Preparing the Church Building for Lent

In *The Ceremonies of the Eucharist* Howard Galley writes:

> During Lent, it is desirable that the church itself reflect the austerity of the season. Where there is a mural or picture behind the altar (and it is not a representation of the crucifixion), it is appropriately concealed from view by a veil of a color that does not call attention to itself. Banners and other decorations (including pictures) are

---

1. New York: Church Hymnal Corporation, 1990; edited by Ann E. McElligott for the Office of Evangelism Ministries of the Episcopal Church.

appropriately removed and the use of flowers avoided. Ornate candlesticks are suitably replaced by simpler ones, and the use of a special processional cross is appropriate. Medieval Lenten processional crosses were generally of wood, stained or painted a deep red, and usually were not crucifixes.[2]

The Sarum Lenten array—off-white or "unbleached linen" vestments and frontal, with matching veils for statues and crosses—is increasingly being used in place of violet during Lent. There is no theological implication in the use of one or the other. Galley recommends the Sarum Lenten color for frontals and veils, but not for vestments. In many churches it will be appropriate to leave a free-standing altar with no frontal during Lent.

Sarum Lenten veils and frontals were traditionally marked in deep red or black with some appropriate symbol (such as the crown of thorns or instruments of the passion). Triptychs were closed. Veils covering crosses which were not removed were usually marked with a simple Latin cross and crown of thorns. Many today use no ornamentation, so that no attention is called to the veiled objects. The use of a Lenten processional cross, as described by Galley above, is preferable to veiling the usual processional cross.

The question of veiling crosses during Lent (or during Holy Week) requires rethinking. Certainly the veiling or removal of a jeweled cross or triumphant *Christus Rex* is consistent with Lenten austerity, but wooden crosses or crucifixes which accent the central themes of the season probably should remain visible. Sarum custom veiled the crosses as part of the Lenten array. Modern Roman use confines the veiling to Holy Week. There is no reason to continue the medieval Roman tradition of veiling crosses for "Passiontide," the final two weeks of Lent.

Some, including Galley, exempt the Fourth Sunday in Lent, traditionally called *Laetare* Sunday (from the Latin introit) or Refreshment Sunday (from the gospel account of the feeding of the five thousand, now read

---

2. Galley, *Ceremonies of the Eucharist*, 42.

---

only in Year B), from the Lenten austerity. They permit the use of flowers and more elaborate vestments on this day.

2. Lenten Liturgy

Some parishes believe that Rite One is preferable to Rite Two during Lent. In fact, Rite Two, with Eucharistic Prayer A or C, is equally suitable for Lent, and the decision of which rite to use is one which can be made in the light of the traditions and needs of the particular congregation.

During Lent, Alleluias are not used, and are omitted in those places in the liturgy in which they occur at other seasons. This is true even on major feasts in Lent. *Gradual Psalms* provides a tract, or alternatively a verse of Scripture, which may be sung instead of the Alleluia before the gospel. A tract is a psalm, or portion of a psalm, sung straight through, without antiphon or refrain, and is the traditional Lenten substitute for use during the gospel procession. The only apparent exception to the suppression of the Alleluia is the burial rite, where the Easter character of the liturgy prevails, especially in the *kontakion* in the commendation and in the acclamation, "Alleluia. Christ is risen."

Gloria in excelsis is not used during Lent, except on festivals. If it is used only on the Annunciation, it will sharply distinguish this major feast of our Lord, on which the Lenten fast is suspended (BCP 17), from the rest of Lent. There is a proper opening acclamation for Lent, "Bless the Lord who forgives all our sins" (BCP 351). An authorized alternative from *Supplementary Liturgical Materials* is

> *Celebrant*   Blessed be the God of our salvation:
> *People*   Who bears our burdens and forgives our sins.

The use of the Penitential Order at the beginning of the liturgy or the occasional substitution of the Great Litany for all that precedes the collect are appropriate Lenten options. When the Great Litany is used, the Prayers of the People are omitted.

There is a long-standing difference of opinion about the most appropriate place for a Confession of Sin in the Lenten liturgy.[3] Some feel that the use of the Penitential Order provides an appropriate penitential introduction to Lenten liturgy. Others prefer to keep the Confession of Sin as a response to the word and introduction to the sacrament and begin the liturgy with the Lenten acclamation, the Collect for Purity, and the *Trisagion* or *Kyrie*. In one place or the other the Confession of Sin should form a regular part of Lenten liturgies, although it may reasonably be omitted when the Great Litany is used.

The Great Litany is best sung in procession to the music at S 67 in *The Hymnal 1982*. It concludes with the *Kyrie*, which may be sung to any appropriate setting, at the end of which the presider sings the salutation ("The Lord be with you") and the collect of the day. The procession should go around the church, if necessary more than once. It need not begin from the altar. Ideally the procession, led by cross and torchbearers, includes the choir and congregation as well as the liturgical ministers, the presider walking last. The congregation join the procession as it moves through the church. In many places there is insufficient space for the congregation to join the procession, and only the choir, servers, and clergy process. This may be necessary, but it is not as effective as having everyone process. The singing of the Litany is in no way restricted to clergy, and it is usually desirable to have a member of the choir serve as cantor. The cantor walks directly behind the processional cross. It is proper for the cantor to wear a cope, but the usual choir dress is equally appropriate. If incense is used in the procession, the thurifer precedes the cross.

The *Agnus Dei* suitably replaces the anthem "Christ our Passover" at the fraction during Lent, or one of the proper *Confractoria*, or fraction anthems, from *The Book of Occasional Services* (BOS 17-19) may be sung.

---

3. See Galley, *Ceremonies of the Eucharist*, 77.

Music for most of them is in *The Hymnal 1982*. *Confractorium* 6, "Whoever believes in me shall not hunger or thirst, for the bread which I give for the life of the world is my flesh," is especially appropriate for Lent 4 in Year B.

The Book of Occasional Services contains a solemn Prayer over the People to be used in place of a seasonal blessing during Lent (BOS 24-26). The deacon (or the presider, if there is no deacon) says (or sings), "Bow down before the Lord," the people kneel or bow, and the priest says (or sings) the prayer with hands extended over the congregation. Five numbered prayers are provided, as well as prayers to be used on Ash Wednesday and in Holy Week. The prayer for Ash Wednesday may be used on Ash Wednesday and the days following, the prayer for Lent I during the first full week of Lent, and so forth. The use of the Prayer over the People is always optional. It may simply be omitted in Rite Two, or the traditional blessing used in Rite One or Rite Two.

The Lenten canticle *Kyrie Pantokrator* (Canticle 14) may be included in the eucharist during Lent. It may be used in place of an entrance hymn, giving a distinctive Lenten beginning to the liturgy, or it may be sung (or said) between the New Testament reading and the gospel, instead of a tract or hymn. If the daily office is not regularly sung in the church, this may be the only opportunity for the congregation to become acquainted with this penitential canticle.

The wider spectrum of description of Lenten endeavors in the second Lenten proper preface suggests its use except for the First Sunday in Lent, when the temptation in the wilderness is the gospel theme.

Collects and eucharistic readings for the weekdays of Lent are included in *Lesser Feasts and Fasts*. The proper consists of a collect, an Old Testament reading, a gradual (or responsorial) psalm, and a gospel reading. "Where there is not a daily celebration of the Eucharist, the Proper appointed for any weekday may be used on any other weekday in the same week" (LFF 28). If there are only one or two weekday eucharists, it is worthwhile picking the readings most appropriate for the occasion from among the available choices. In principle Lenten weekdays are given preference to lesser feasts:

In keeping with ancient tradition, the observance of Lenten weekdays ordinarily takes precedence over Lesser Feasts occurring during this season. It is, appropriate, however, to name the saint whose day it is in the Prayers of the People, and, if desired, to use the Collect of the saint to conclude the Prayers. (LFF 28)

The ordinary pattern is to *celebrate* only St. Matthias, St. Joseph, and the Annunciation—the three major feasts—during Lent, using the Lenten weekday propers on all other days. Lesser feasts are *commemorated* as indicated, by mentioning the name of the saint during the Prayers of the People and, if convenient, using the proper collect as the concluding prayer of the Prayers of the People. The name of the saint may also be included in the intercessions in Eucharistic Prayer D.

The rule is not so strict as to actually forbid the celebration of lesser feasts. Obviously a patronal festival is celebrated as a major feast, and may be transferred to any convenient day in the week. The day on which a regular midweek Lenten service is held is an appropriate occasion, so that the greatest number of people can participate. Other lesser feasts which might be celebrated rather than commemorated in particular places include St. David (March 1), St. Patrick (March 17), and Martin Luther King, Jr. (April 4).

The Lenten hangings may be kept in place even on the major feasts. If a festal frontal and flowers are used only on the Annunciation, it will help to set that major feast of our Lord apart from Lenten weekdays, as the Prayer Book calendar implies (BCP 17).

3. Catechumenal Rites

The use of the rites during Lent for the preparation of candidates for baptism and of baptized persons for the reaffirmation of the baptismal covenant at Easter is optional, although it is the preparation of catechumens for baptism which creates the particular Lenten character of the season. When the catechumenal rites are used during Lent, the bishop may permit the use of the Year A propers during Lent and Eastertide (BOS 128). These are the classic Johannine "signs" which provided the traditional texts for the catechumenate. A series of homilies on these texts offers a basic course in Christian faith and life.

a. Enrollment of Candidates

The Enrollment of Candidates for Baptism at the Great Vigil of Easter normally takes place on the First Sunday in Lent (BOS 122). A large book is needed in which the candidates sign their names. This may be a parish register which has places to record the names of catechumens, or it may be a separate book for the purpose. The book "is placed where it can be easily seen and used." Its symbolism is that as the names of the candidates are written in the book in the sanctuary, so may God write their names in the Book of Life (BOS 123). The book may be placed on the altar before the beginning of the service. In many churches it will be both convenient and appropriate for the candidates to come to the altar to sign their names. In places with long chancels, it may be preferable to bring the book to a table or stand at the chancel step to be signed. The bishop, the bishop's representative, or the rector (or priest-in-charge) presides (BOS 116).

After the creed the catechumens to be enrolled and their sponsors come forward. If the catechumens stand together in a line on the south side of the aisle with their sponsors behind them and the presider faces them from the north side, it will provide better visual lines for the congregation than if the catechumens and sponsors stand with their backs to the congregation; the physical layout of a particular church may suggest other arrangements. "A Catechist, or other lay representative of the congregation, presents them to the bishop or priest" (BOS 122). Ideally, the catechist who has taken the leading role in preparing the catechumens should present them for enrollment, but if that is not possible another appropriate lay member of the congregation may do so. The presider asks the two questions of the sponsors, asks the congregation if they approve of enrolling the catechumens as candidates, and asks the catechumens if they desire to be baptized. The presider then says the form admitting them as candidates, and the candidates write their names in the book. If the book is to be signed on the altar, the presider goes to the altar. If the book is to be placed on a stand or table so that the signing may be plainly seen, the presider should stand across the table or stand facing the candidates. A deacon brings the book from the altar and places it where it is to be signed. The deacon stands beside the book, pointing to the place for each to sign and generally giving assistance.

If the sponsors are also to sign the book, they sign after the candidate has signed. The candidates read their names aloud as they write them. If a candidate is unable to write, the deacon or the sponsor may write the name while the candidate says it aloud.

The candidates and sponsors remain together at the front of the church while a deacon leads the litany (BOS 124-125). If there is no deacon, an assisting priest or a lay person leads the litany. The presider says the final prayer with hands extended over the candidates. The candidates kneel, or bow their heads. All should follow their example.

The candidates return to their place and the liturgy continues with the Confession of Sin (unless it was used in the Penitential Order) or with the Peace (BOS 126).

b. The Lenten Scrutinies

By the beginning of the sixth century three Lenten scrutinies, on the Third, Fourth, and Fifth Sundays in Lent, were so well-established in Rome that questions could be asked about their meaning. Originally they were principal catechetical occasions. The gospel readings were traditionally the

Samaritan woman (John 4), the man born blind (John 9), and the raising of Lazarus (John 11), our selections for Year A.

The section During Candidacy in *The Book of Occasional Services* contains three prayers and three blessings of the candidates to be used on these occasions, although it does not use the term scrutinies (BOS 126-127). If these prayers are used, the candidates and their sponsors are called forward by the deacon before the Prayers of the People. The candidates kneel or bow their heads. The sponsors each place a hand on the shoulder of their candidate.

Using the form in the book, the presider bids the people to pray in silence. After a period of silent prayer, the presider says one of the prayers appointed. The first prayer and blessing can be used at the first scrutiny, and the second and third the two following weeks. After the prayer the presider in silence lays a hand on the head of each candidate. The blessing is said with hands extended over all the candidates. They return to their places and the liturgy continues with the Prayers of the People. If it is the custom of the parish to dismiss catechumens from the Sunday eucharist (BOS 128), the candidates leave following their blessing.

The Book of Occasional Services also states:

> It is appropriate that the Apostles' (or Nicene) Creed be given to the Candidates for Baptism on the Third Sunday in Lent and the Lord's Prayer be given to them on the Fifth Sunday in Lent. (This may follow the Prayers for the Candidates for Baptism on those Sundays.) (BOS 128)

These are the ancient ceremonies of the *traditio symboli* and *traditio orationis* which are found in the writings of the fourth-century church fathers. Their purpose was to teach the words of the creed, which formed an outline of the instruction and to which the candidates would be asked to assent at baptism, and of the Lord's Prayer, which was recited in the liturgy after the catechumens had been dismissed. The candidates were told not to write these things down, but to learn them by heart. Immediately before baptism the candidates "returned" the creed, reciting it aloud before the congregation.

A form for doing this was added to the 1994 edition of *The Book of Occasional Services*. Immediately after the sermon the candidates and sponsors are called forward. The prayers for the candidates for baptism are then said. On the Third Sunday in Lent the candidates remain kneeling or with heads bowed to receive the creed. The sponsors place a hand upon the shoulder of their candidate, and one of the catechists says, "Let the candidate(s) for Baptism now receive the Creed from the Church" (BOS 129). The people and presider recite the creed, all standing. One additional possibility, following ancient traditions and the Roman Catholic RCIA, is to address the candidates immediately before beginning the creed. A traditional address is similar to this:

> Brothers and sisters, hear the words of the creed which proclaim the faith of the church. Write them in your heart, and confess them with your lips. For St. Paul says, "One believes with the heart and so is justified, and one confesses with the mouth and so is saved."

The presider then begins the creed, and the congregation joins in. The Apostles' Creed is most traditional, but either creed may be used. The presider then may dismiss the candidates, and they and their sponsors return to their places.

Similarly, on the Fifth Sunday in Lent the Lord's Prayer is given. One of the catechists asks that the candidates "now receive the Lord's Prayer from the Church," and the presider introduces the Lord's Prayer as it is introduced in the eucharist, in either the traditional or contemporary form. The congregation recite the Lord's Prayer. The presider may then dismiss the candidates and all return to their places (BOS 129-130).

Both of these rites are purely optional and need not be a part of the scrutinies. They may also be used without the scrutinies. They are intended to give ritual expression to the instruction in faith and prayer which the candidates are receiving, and to emphasize the important place of believing and praying in Christian life.

4. Other Services in Lent

Lent is also a season in which many congregations schedule additional midweek services to give parishioners an opportunity to engage in "special acts of discipline and self-denial." These services may be of many types: midweek eucharists, the Order of Worship for the Evening, Morning or Evening Prayer, Noonday Prayer, Compline, mission or preaching services, sacred concerts, or the Way of the Cross. A decision about which, if any, of these services are appropriate is a part of the Lenten planning for individual congregations. Churches in downtown business districts may wish to schedule noontime eucharists, preaching services, or organ recitals. Those in residential communities will probably consider evening services. Important as these extra services often are in the congregation's observance of Lent, the primary Lenten observance is at the Sunday eucharists. Prayer, fasting, and almsgiving do not always require liturgical assemblies.

a. An Order of Worship for the Evening

The Order of Worship for the Evening with a sermon after the reading makes an excellent midweek evening service for congregations not familiar with singing the daily office. It is appropriate any evening in Lent except during Holy Week. It is a good contemporary example of the parochial or "cathedral" office.

The congregation assemble in a darkened church. A lighted candle or lamp is carried in, by a deacon or the officiant. It is placed in a standing candlestick near the altar, or on the altar (if it is a smaller candle). The officiant says or sings the Lenten opening acclamation, "Bless the Lord who forgives all our sins." The short lesson is omitted, or a reader reads 1 John 1:5-7. The officiant says or sings the Lenten Prayer for Light (BCP 111). The altar candles are lighted, and the lighting in the church turned on. This may be done in silence, or the Lenten *lucernarium* (anthem) from *The Book of Occasional Services* (BOS 13) may be sung. Music is at S 312 in the Appendix to *The Hymnal 1982* (Accompaniment Edition Volume 1). Note that *The Book of Common Prayer* appears to place the *lucernarium* after the Prayer for Light, but the structure of the *lucernarium*, ending with a versicle and response, suggests that the prayer should follow it.

The evening hymn *Phos hilaron* or a proper Lenten substitute for it is sung. The candle and the congregation may be censed during the hymn (BCP 143). The psalm and lesson which follow are not taken from the course reading of the lectionary and are chosen for their appropriateness. Evening psalms, such as 141, are particularly appropriate. The sermon follows the reading. The *Magnificat*, or a metrical version thereof, or some other canticle or hymn of praise is sung.

A litany such as Suffrages B for Evening Prayer is said or sung. If it is sung, the versicles may be sung by a cantor or the officiant. The officiant introduces the Lord's Prayer, and says or sings the collect of the day, or another appropriate collect. If the officiant is a priest, the Aaronic blessing follows. The deacon or officiant dismisses the people with a dismissal, as at the eucharist. The service may conclude with the exchange of the Peace.

b. *The Way of the Cross*

The Way of the Cross is also appropriate as a midweek Lenten service, especially on the Fridays of Lent. A text is included in *The Book of Occasional Services* (BOS 57-73). The service dates from the time of the Crusades, and, like the classic Holy Week rites, seeks to copy what was done in Jerusalem; in this case, it is the offering of prayer by pilgrims at various sites along the path walked by Jesus carrying the cross to Golgotha. It may be used as a private devotion, or as a corporate meditation, with reflections on each of the stations. It is traditionally conducted as a procession with stops (or stations) at wooden crosses on the walls of the church. Often, in addition to the crosses, there are pictures or other representations of the events being commemorated. Sometimes the stations are not placed around the walls of the church, but are in a cloister, or outdoors in a garden. Extensive directions are given in the section Concerning the Service in *The Book of Occasional Services* (BOS 56). The service in *The Book of Occasional Services* includes the traditional fourteen stations. Only eight are based directly on events recorded in the gospels, and the nonbiblical stations (3, 4, 6, 7, 9, and 13) may be omitted.

The officiant may be a bishop, priest, deacon, or lay person. The officiant leads the congregation around the church, stopping at the various stations for prayer. A reader reads a brief description of the event commemorated at each station. The procession is appropriately led by someone carrying a wooden cross in front of the officiant. This may be the Lenten processional cross. If crucifer and officiant wear vestments, cassock and surplice, or alb are appropriate.

The Book of Occasional Services points out correctly that the hymn *Stabat Mater* (Hymn 159) frequently associated with the Way of the Cross is not integral to it, and any suitable hymn of the passion may be used. The form included uses the *Trisagion* as a chant while the procession moves from station to station.

A hymn may be sung during the entrance of the liturgical ministers. They stand before the altar, and the officiant leads the opening devotions. The procession then goes to the first station. A hymn verse may be sung during this procession. At each station the officiant says the opening versicle, the reader reads the description of the station, the officiant says a proper versicle, "Let us pray," and, after a pause for silent prayer, the collect for that station. If the *Trisagion* is not sung between the stations, it is then recited and a hymn verse sung as the procession moves to the next station.

During the singing of the *Trisagion* after the last station, the procession returns to the center and the officiant stands before the altar to lead the concluding prayers. After the final prayer, the ministers leave the sanctuary in silence.

The Way of the Cross may be readily adapted for use in spaces that lack the room for a procession from station to station. The service may be conducted with only the officiant and a crucifer going from station to station, and the congregation remaining in their places. More imaginatively, it may be conducted as a meditative service, with representations of the stations projected on the wall or on a screen, with time for reflection before the singing of the *Trisagion*.

HOLY
WEEK

Chapter Three

The Rites of Holy Week

Holy Week is generally believed to have developed in Jerusalem in the fourth century during the episcopate of the great bishop and preacher St. Cyril. The Easter Vigil was already in existence, and the combination of a heightened interest in Christian history, the construction of churches on the sacred sites in the Holy Land by Constantine, and the influx of pilgrims to Jerusalem for Easter produced the series of services that became our Holy Week. These services were usually held in Jerusalem on the original sites and at the times indicated in the gospels. The Spanish pilgrim Egeria, who visited Jerusalem in the 380s, was fascinated by the novel celebration of what they called Great Week and described the services in detail in her journal.[1] She was particularly impressed that the psalms and readings were appropriate to the time and place—obviously a new idea to her.

---

1. Portions of her writings appear in Wright, *Readings for the Daily Office.*

Whether the Holy Week liturgies were invented by Cyril or borrowed from other churches, it was from Jerusalem that pilgrims took them home, adapting and incorporating them into the liturgical cycle of their own churches. These rites thus provided the basic structure of the liturgical celebrations of Holy Week. Kenneth Stevenson calls the piety of these rites "rememorative": they remember the historical events of the passion.[2] They do not imitate them like a passion play, but they are remembered symbolically so that we may enter into them. The gospel story is the thread on which the events hang, and we move with Christ from event to event throughout the week.

In the later Middle Ages the rites were again embellished, both to reflect the piety of the period and to incorporate new ideas brought by the Crusaders, such as the Stations of the Cross. This is the period in which dramatic additions were made to the rites, such as burying the cross or a consecrated host in the Easter sepulchre, or carrying a coffin for the body of Christ in the Good Friday liturgy. Stevenson refers to this as "representational" piety. The difference between the two pieties is reflected in Christian art in the evolution of the crucifix from a representation of the Christ reigning from the tree to the realistic portrayal of the dying Jesus with drops of blood coming from his hands and side. These two pieties can also be seen in hymns such as "Sing, my tongue, the glorious battle," an early hymn traditionally sung during the Good Friday liturgy at the veneration of the cross, and the seventeenth-century "O sacred head, sore wounded." The Reformation produced even further changes, as most of the classical rites disappeared and the cross-centered piety of the late Middle Ages remained.

Finally, in the twentieth century there has been a revival of the classic rites. They were first reintroduced to Anglicanism in the nineteenth century in their late medieval Roman or Sarum form, but it was not until the middle

----

2. Kenneth Stevenson, *Jerusalem Revisited: The Liturgical Meaning of Holy Week* (Washington, D.C.: Pastoral Press, 1988), pp. 9ff.

of the twentieth century that they came into widespread use. The Society of St. John the Evangelist published *An American Holy Week Manual* in 1946. In 1954 the Roman Catholic Church published in Latin a "restoration" of the Holy Week liturgies, and these were subsequently translated into English in the reforms following Vatican Council II. In 1958 a second revised edition of *An American Holy Week Manual*, edited by Earle H. Maddux, SSJE, appeared, including "the recently revised texts of the Holy Week Liturgy." In the same year Massey Shepherd edited *Holy Week Offices* for Associated Parishes; it was published by Seabury Press under the auspices of the Adult Division of the Department of Christian Education. This collection represented a serious attempt to adapt the traditional Holy Week liturgies for use in the mainstream of Episcopal Churches. The 1960 edition of *The Book of Offices*, an official publication, included a Palm Sunday blessing of palms and an Easter Even blessing of the paschal candle. All of this led to the inclusion of proper liturgies for Holy Week in *Prayer Book Studies 19* in 1970, and then in *The Book of Common Prayer*.

1. Holy Week Today

Holy Week remains an important devotional and liturgical occasion for Episcopalians. *The Book of Common Prayer* contains propers for the offices for every day and for the celebration of the eucharist daily through Maundy Thursday, as well as proper liturgies for Palm Sunday, Maundy Thursday, Good Friday, Holy Saturday, and the Great Vigil of Easter. The Way of the Cross and Tenebrae are included in *The Book of Occasional Services*. Holy Week is also the occasion for other devotional and quasi-liturgical services, as well as sacred concerts and passion plays. The desire to reach as many people as possible with the proclamation of the death and resurrection of Christ and our participation in it has given rise to a wide variety of services and religious activities, both individual and corporate. The proper liturgies of Palm Sunday, Maundy Thursday, and Good Friday reflect the rememorative piety of late antiquity, although we tend to interpret them through the representational piety of later ages. The collect appointed to be used during the Palm Sunday procession well expresses the piety with which we enter Holy Week:

> Mercifully grant that we, walking in the way of the cross, may find it none other than the way of life and peace. (BCP 272)

Most parishes do not have the resources to do everything which could conceivably be done. The primary foci are Easter, the Great Vigil, the Palm Sunday liturgy, the Maundy Thursday eucharist, and the Good Friday liturgy. Then other services should be scheduled and planned, according to interest, available resources to do them well, and parish custom.

The liturgical color for Holy Week is red. Traditional Holy Week vestments have been of an oxblood shade with black orphreys. Red vestments clearly designed for Pentecost with tongues of fire or similar symbols are not appropriate. An altar frontal matching the vestments may be used, or the Lenten frontal may be left in place until the stripping of the altar on Maundy Thursday, if the color does not clash with the vestments.

Eucharistic propers with three lessons for Monday, Tuesday, and Wednesday are in the Prayer Book lectionary. A proper Prayer over the People for use in place of the blessing from Palm Sunday through Maundy Thursday is found among the seasonal blessings in *The Book of Occasional Services* (BOS 26). The collect of the day is used at the offices throughout the week.

2. The Triduum

The Latin word *triduum* means a period of three days. It is used neither in *The Book of Common Prayer* nor in *The Book of Occasional Services*, yet it is widely used by Episcopalians and needs to be mentioned. It refers to the period beginning with sundown on Maundy Thursday and extending until sundown on Easter. It corresponds to the ancient celebration of the *Pascha*, with two days of fasting and one of celebration. It includes, therefore, the Maundy Thursday eucharist, the Good Friday liturgy, the Holy Saturday Word liturgy, the Great Vigil of Easter, and the services on Easter Day.

The advantage of the concept from a theological and liturgical point of view is that it restores a measure of the unitive nature of the paschal celebration. We begin with the celebration of the eucharist commemorating the Lord's Supper, with its remembrance of the institution of the sacrament and the washing of feet. This celebration is tied to the Good Friday liturgy, so that the institution of the eucharist is directly related to Christ's death on the cross, and both are related to the celebration of the resurrection at the Great Vigil and in the services of Easter Day. Ormonde Plater has pointed out that the omission of the dismissal at the Maundy Thursday and Good Friday liturgies also serves to tie the liturgies of the Triduum together. In one sense it is a single liturgical act, from Maundy Thursday through the Great Vigil. This is the period in which we pass over with Christ from death to life, celebrating each event in the drama of salvation and entering into the mystery of dying and rising again with the Lord of life. It is here that all of the pieties of Holy Week come together, and at many different levels the people of God are caught up into the divine mystery. We die, and live and reign with Christ.

Chapter Four

Palm Sunday

The double title of Palm Sunday in the Prayer Book, "The Sunday of the Passion: Palm Sunday," well describes the liturgy of the day. The Liturgy of the Palms, with its triumphal procession, modulates into a penitential eucharist dominated by the solemn proclamation of the passion gospel. The two themes should not be mixed. Triumphal hymns are not sung after the beginning of the eucharist. If the choir wishes to sing a Palm Sunday anthem it may be sung either during the distribution of the palms or in place of the opening anthem of the Liturgy of the Palms. The altar may be decorated with palm branches. *The Book of Common Prayer, The Altar Book,* and *The Hymnal 1982* contain the necessary texts and music. Music for singing the passion gospels is available from many sources: Mason Martens has set the traditional music to the *Revised Standard Version* texts and Ormonde Plater to the *New Revised Standard Version* texts.

The liturgy begins in a location other than the church, such as the parish hall, where the people may gather and set out in procession to the church. Carrying the palm branches in procession into the church in celebration of Christ's triumphal entry into Jerusalem is the purpose of blessing the palms, so the procession should be impressive and involve everyone in the congregation able to participate. It is highly desirable to give those unable to walk in the procession a part in it by using the sound system to allow those who must wait in the church to hear the Liturgy of the Palms, or by providing them a shorter route from the parish hall into the church to await the procession's arrival. The vestments for Palm Sunday are red. The presider may wear a cope, changing to the chasuble at the end of the procession, or a chasuble may be worn throughout. Unless the changing of vesture is integral to the rite, as when the newly baptized put on white robes, it is best done as inconspicuously as possible.

Although the use of imported palm branches has become customary in the United States, the older tradition was to use local trees or shrubs, such as evergreens, palmettos, or pussy willows, in places where palms did not grow. Palm crosses are unsuitable for carrying in the procession and confuse the two aspects of the celebration, the triumphal entry and the passion. The branches need to be prepared for distribution and placed on a table where the blessing will take place. Alternatively, ushers may distribute the palms to the congregation on their arrival. The people then hold up their palms during the blessing, avoiding the need to distribute them before the procession.

1. The Palm Sunday Liturgy

a. The Liturgy of the Palms

The Liturgy of the Palms precedes the principal eucharist. The clergy and people gather in the parish house or elsewhere (outdoors in suitable climates). The liturgical ministers are vested for the eucharist. The presider may wear a cope or chasuble. The crucifer and torchbearers stand together behind the presider, facing the congregation, or in some other convenient place. The presider faces the congregation across the table holding the

palms, if that is possible. The liturgy begins with "Blessed is the King...."
This may be sung or said as a versicle and response between the presider
and congregation, or a cantor may sing the versicle. Alternatively, the
anthem, or another suitable anthem, may be sung by the choir. If a more
extensive anthem begins the service, "Blessed is the King..." may be used
as an opening acclamation at its close.

The presider sings or says the collect. The acolyte or deacon may hold
the book. The deacon then sings or reads the gospel of the triumphal entry,
with the usual announcement, conclusion, and responses. The ceremonial
customary at the Sunday eucharist is followed. If there is no deacon,
someone else may sing or read the gospel, either in the manner of a
eucharistic gospel or as a lesson.

The blessing of the palms is similar to a eucharistic preface, introduced
by the traditional dialogue and sung to the traditional music, which is in
The Altar Book. The presider stands with hands in the orans position facing
the people. No particular ceremonial actions are necessary. The sign of the
cross may be made over the branches at "Let these branches be for us..."
and the presider may sprinkle them with holy water and cense them at the
conclusion of the prayer. If the palms for the people were distributed prior
to the services, the people should hold them during the blessing.

The anthem *Benedictus qui venit* may be sung by the choir during the
distribution, or used as a versicle and response following the blessing. The
distribution should be as expeditious as possible. Clergy, acolytes, and
ushers may all take part. If the people have already received their palms,
the presider should give palms to the deacon(s) and other liturgical
ministers.

b. The Procession
When the palms have been distributed, the procession is formed. If incense
is used, the thurifer leads the procession, followed by the cross and torches.
The choir and congregation follow, with assisting clergy, liturgical minis-

ters, deacon(s), and presider at the end. When all is ready a deacon sings or says, "Let us go forth in peace."

The traditional hymn during the procession is "All glory, laud, and honor" (Hymn 154/155). The verses may be sung by the choir, or sections of the choir, with the congregation joining in the refrain. Other suitable hymns, such as "Ride on! ride on in majesty!" (Hymn 156) may be included. Psalm 118:19-29 is quoted in the biblical account of the triumphal entry, and may also be sung. A station may be made at the entrance to the church, or some other appropriate place. The presider sings or says the collect given for the purpose in the Prayer Book, beginning the transition to the Sunday of the Passion. The procession resumes. The psalm or one of the hymns is sung. When the procession arrives in the sanctuary all go to their places. The presider, either at the chair or standing before the altar, faces the people and sings "The Lord be with you" and the collect for the day. The Palm Sunday procession is now over and the eucharist of the Sunday of the Passion has begun.

c. The Lessons and Passion Gospel

The Old Testament reading, Psalm 22, and the epistle follow. If a hymn is used before the passion gospel, a Holy Week hymn, such as "O sacred head, sore wounded" is appropriate, or the verse or tract from *Gradual Psalms* may be used.

The passion gospel is the distinctive element of the eucharist for this day. It is from the reading of the gospel narrative of the suffering and death of Jesus that the Sunday derives the name Sunday of the Passion. Originally the account of the passion and resurrection of Christ were read as the gospel at the Great Vigil of Easter, but even before Holy Week developed in the fourth century, the passion narrative became attached to the Sunday before Easter. In Rome the account from the Gospel of Matthew was read on that Sunday. Wednesday and Friday were the traditional station days on which there were midweek liturgies, and other passion narratives were used on them to reprise the Sunday theme. When the celebration of mass daily during Holy Week became customary, the passion narrative from Mark was assigned to Tuesday, Luke to Wednesday, and John to Friday.

The Anglican Prayer Books divided up the long passion gospels, assigning Mark to Monday and Tuesday, and Luke to Wednesday and Thursday. The first part of the Matthew and John passions were assigned as the second lesson for Morning Prayer on Palm Sunday and Good Friday respectively. With the adoption of the three-year lectionary in the 1979 Prayer Book, the synoptic passion narratives were assigned to Palm Sunday (Matthew to Year A, Mark to Year B, and Luke to Year C), while John remained on Good Friday every year. The lectionary permits the use of a shortened form of the passion, but the reading of the entire account, at least at the principal eucharist, is highly desirable.

Traditionally the passion gospel has been sung by three deacons, but many alternative methods of presenting the sacred story have developed in the last half-century. Probably the least effective is for a single reader to read the passion like other Sunday gospels. The distinctiveness of its presentation underscores the distinctive content of the passion gospel. The passion gospel may be read responsively or sung. It is appropriate for a deacon to read the narrator's part, and for the presider to read the words of Jesus, but neither is necessary. There may be as few as three readers, a single reader taking the parts of all the other persons, or different readers may take the part of each person. Sometimes four readers are used, a man reading (or singing) the men's parts, and a woman the women's parts. The readers need not be ordained and may be recruited from the choir or congregation. If the passion is sung, vocal ability rather than ecclesiastical office is the chief qualification. It is important that the readers rehearse their parts, whether the text is read or sung. The congregation may take the part of the crowd, and it is certainly effective to have the congregation do this, as it includes the shout, "Crucify him!"; for many people this brings the horror of the crucifixion home to them. Texts need to be provided for the people if they are to act as the crowd, including music for their lines, if the passion is sung. As mentioned above, Ormonde Plater's *Passion Gospels* sets the *New Revised Standard Version* texts to the traditional music. There are innumerable other settings of the passion, including many by classical composers. The proclamation of the passion is the gospel of the day, not a sacred concert, however, and the communication of the text is the primary consideration in choosing how it is to be done.

Neither lights nor incense is used for the reading of the passion. There is a special form of announcement: "The Passion of our Lord Jesus Christ according to _____." The readers go to their places during the hymn or tract. The narrator goes to the pulpit or lectern, the other readers stand where they can be seen and heard. Readers who are members of the congregation wear their ordinary clothes. The congregation may sit until the mention of the arrival at Golgotha, and then stand. The reader pauses in silence after the mention of the death of Christ. All may kneel or bow; the actions of the readers and the presider will signal this to the people. After a moment, the reader resumes, and all stand. At the conclusion of the passion there is no response, and the readers return to their places in silence.

d. The Holy Communion

The sermon follows the reading of the passion gospel. The Nicene Creed and the Confession of Sin are omitted. The eucharist continues as usual. Eucharistic Prayer A with the Holy Week preface is appropriate. After the postcommunion prayer the deacon says or sings, "Bow down before the Lord," and the presider sings the Holy Week Prayer over the People from *The Book of Occasional Services* (BOS 26), if it is used. The deacon dismisses the people.

2. Other Palm Sunday Liturgies

If there are additional liturgies on Palm Sunday, some form of the Liturgy of the Palms is a part of all of them. A simple form is for the ushers to distribute palms to the congregation as they enter the church. The people then hold their palms for the gospel of the triumphal entry and blessing. They sing "All glory, laud, and honor," or recite Psalm 118:19-29, while the presider and liturgical ministers proceed to the sanctuary. If a fuller form is desired, they may follow the suggestions for small congregations in the next section.

3. Palm Sunday in Small Congregations

The Liturgy of the Palms and the reading of the passion provide opportunities in a small congregation for everyone to participate actively in the service. Every effort must be made to make it possible for the congregation to join in the procession and to read the part of the crowd in the passion. Different readers may be used for the gospel of the triumphal entry, the eucharistic lessons, and the various voices of the passion, involving a number of lay people. If the choir is small, a single voice, a cantor, may lead the singing. If the congregation are accustomed to singing the *sursum corda* at the eucharist, they can sing the responses (Hymn 153) at the blessing of the palms. If the presider is accustomed to singing the eucharistic preface, he or she may sing the blessing.

The congregation gather in the parish house, or in some other convenient place (outdoors in warm climates), or if that is not possible, in the narthex of the church. If nothing else is possible the congregation may gather in the church itself and the palms may be placed on a table at the back of the nave. The opening anthem may be said, or the choir (or cantor) may lead its singing. The presider says the collect, and a reader reads the gospel narrative of the triumphal entry, holding the book. If there is a deacon or assisting priest, he or she reads the gospel as a eucharistic gospel with the usual ceremony and responses. The presider says the blessing of the palms facing the congregation across the table on which the palms are placed. If the congregation already have the palms, they hold them during the blessing. The presider may make the sign of the cross at the words "Let these branches...." The presider holds the book with both hands during the collect and blessing, except while making the sign of the cross. If someone else holds the book, the presider stands in the orans position. At the conclusion of the blessing, the *Benedictus qui venit* is sung to any familiar tune. If the palms have not been distributed before the service, the presider, acolytes, and ushers distribute them during the singing.

When all have received their palms, the crucifer leads the congregation into the church. If there are torchbearers, they accompany the crucifer. If the congregation has gathered in the narthex, the procession moves down the center aisle. At least the children and the choir can process, carrying palms, in even the smallest space. The hymn "All glory, laud, and honor" is sung during the procession. At the end of the hymn, the priest says "The Lord be with you" and the collect of the day, facing the congregation from the sanctuary. Music and texts used during the rest of the service emphasize the passion, not the triumphal entry. The eucharist continues with the readings. A hymn of the passion may be sung before the passion gospel.

The passion gospel is read by readers chosen from the choir and congregation. The presider may read the words of Jesus, but it is not necessary. The narrator, who may be the deacon, stands at the lectern. The other readers stand wherever it is convenient, as long as they can be heard. Texts of the passion indicating the crowd part for them to take are distributed to the congregation on arrival. It is customary for the reader to pause briefly after reading the account of the death of Christ. All may kneel or bow. At the conclusion of the passion the readers return to their places, and the sermon follows.

The Nicene Creed and the Confession of Sin are omitted. The Holy Week Prayer over the People from *The Book of Occasional Services* (BOS 26) may replace the blessing. Otherwise, the service follows the usual Sunday pattern.

---

4. Palm Sunday without a Priest

In the absence of a priest the Liturgy of the Palms may be conducted by a deacon or lay reader. A deacon who presides at the liturgy may wear an alb, dalmatic, and red stole, or an alb or surplice and red stole. A lay reader wears an alb, or cassock and surplice.

All that is said above about gathering elsewhere and processing into the church, and the directions about music apply equally when the presider is not a priest. The presider says the collect and blessing of the palms facing the people, but does not make the sign of the cross or cense or sprinkle the branches. A deacon presider may read the gospel of the triumphal entry, or a lay person may read it as a lesson. After the distribution of the palms, the procession enters the church singing "All glory, laud, and honor." The procession may pause at the church door while the presider says the appointed collect. At the conclusion of the procession the presider goes to the sanctuary or chancel and says the collect of the day, to begin the Liturgy of the Word. The lessons and psalm follow. The passion may be read in the manner described above, with lay persons reading all of the parts. If the presider is not a preacher, a homily may be read.

The Prayers of the People follow the homily. They are led by someone other than the presider, if possible. The presider says the concluding collect and invites the people to exchange the peace.

It will almost always be desirable to follow the Prayer Book's general directions for services "if there is no Communion" by singing a hymn or anthem, taking up a collection and receiving the people's offerings, and concluding the service with the Lord's Prayer and the Grace (BCP 407). The hymn or anthem should focus on the passion, not on the triumphal entry.

If the presider is a deacon, the bishop may authorize the deacon to administer Holy Communion to the congregation from the reserved sacrament (BCP 408). Note that this liturgy is used at the bishop's discretion, not the deacon's. If no priest is available for major celebrations, such as Palm Sunday and Easter, the bishop may allow a resident deacon to distribute communion on those days. Directions for doing so are given in Chapter 11 of Galley's *The Ceremonies of the Eucharist*.

Chapter Five

Monday, Tuesday, and Wednesday in Holy Week

The only special provision for the first three weekdays of Holy Week are eucharistic propers with three lessons and proper collects. No festivals may be observed on any of these days (BCP 17), which gives them a privileged character. Congregations who regularly celebrate the eucharist daily will use these propers, and other congregations may wish to schedule celebrations at convenient hours so that lay people may participate. A proper Prayer over the People for use in place of the blessing is found among the seasonal blessings in *The Book of Occasional Services* (BOS 26). The collect of the day is used at the offices. Sacred concerts, passion plays, and other devotional exercises are frequently scheduled on these days.

1. Tenebrae

Tenebrae is the traditional Latin name for the monastic offices of matins and lauds for the last three days in Holy Week, which, in the Middle Ages, were universally celebrated the evenings before. The distinctive feature from which the name of the service ("darkness" or "shadows") derives is the gradual extinguishing of fourteen candles on a triangular wooden candlestick called a hearse, along with the other lights in the church. The fifteenth candle is hidden while the Good Friday collect is read, symbolizing the crucifixion. A loud noise is made, representing the earthquake at the time of the resurrection (Matthew 28:2), and the hidden light is replaced in the candlestick. The people leave in silence.

As it is conducted today, the service is largely musical.[1] The psalms, responsories, and lessons are sung to traditional tones, or to composed settings. The chant for the lessons from Lamentations is unique. The service in its full form makes considerable musical demands on a choir, and before scheduling Tenebrae it is well to consider whether its celebration will drain too many resources from the more central celebrations of the week.

Since Tenebrae is a form of the daily office, its use in addition to Morning and Evening Prayer represents a duplication of the office for that day.

Although Tenebrae was originally conducted on Wednesday, Thursday, and Friday evenings, *The Book of Occasional Services* provides texts only for Wednesday, "in order that the proper liturgies of Maundy Thursday and Good Friday may find their place as the principal services of those days" (BOS 74). It describes Tenebrae in this form as providing "an extended meditation upon, and a prelude to, the events of our Lord's life between the Last Supper and the Resurrection."

The Book of Occasional Services gives extensive directions for the celebration of Tenebrae. Basically it is conducted as an office from the choir.

---

1. A recent musical edition is *In the Shadow of Holy Week: The Office of Tenebrae*, compiled by Frederick C. Elwood and edited by John L. Hooker (New York: Church Hymnal Corporation, 1996).

The officiant wears cassock and surplice, and, if ordained, may wear a tippet.

In addition to the officiant, a server to extinguish the candles is needed. The tenebrae hearse is traditionally a large triangular wooden candlestick holding fifteen candles. It is placed at the liturgical south of the sanctuary. The altar candles are also lighted. Tenebrae may be done entirely without instrumental accompaniment, and there should be no preludes, postludes, hymns, or other music not a part of the office. No sermon is preached.

The church is decorated for Holy Week. The candles are lighted, including the fifteen candles on the hearse. The choir, clergy, server, and officiant enter in silence, and the service begins at once with the antiphon on the first psalm. All are seated for the psalms (BOS 75). At the conclusion of each psalm the server extinguishes one of the candles on the hearse, beginning on the outside.

The service consists of three Nocturns, with three psalms and three lessons each, the five psalms of Lauds (the fourth psalm is actually a canticle, "The Song of Hezekiah"), the *Benedictus*, Psalm 51, and the Good Friday collect. At the end of each group of psalms there is a versicle and response, all stand for silent prayer, and the reader goes to the lectern. All sit for the lessons. Only the first lesson in each Nocturn is announced and the usual closing formula and response are omitted. The choir may stand to sing the responsories following each lesson, but everyone else remains seated.

At the end of the fifth psalm of Lauds the versicle and response are sung and all stand for the *Benedictus*. During the singing of the *Benedictus* the server extinguishes the altar candles, and all other lights in the church are put out, except for the candle in the center of the hearse. While the antiphon is repeated at the end of the canticle, the server removes the top candle from the hearse and hides it "beneath or behind the Altar, or in some other convenient place" (BOS 89).

All kneel while the anthem "Christ for us became obedient unto death" is sung (or said). After a brief silence Psalm 51 is said (or sung) softly. At its conclusion the officiant says, without chant, the collect as printed in *The*

Book of Occasional Services (BOS 90), without its customary doxology. A noise is made, traditionally by striking two pieces of wood together to make a loud clap, and the candle is brought out and returned to its place. The people leave in silence, the church remaining as dark as possible except for the single candle.

The Book of Occasional Services makes two suggestions for a much shorter service of Tenebrae (BOS 92). Nocturns 2 and 3 and either one or two of the psalms of Lauds are omitted. If one psalm (either 90 or 143) is omitted, then two candles are extinguished at each psalm. If both psalms are omitted, then a seven-branched candlestick is used.

Chapter Six

Maundy Thursday

The name Maundy Thursday is derived from the Latin *mandatum*, and refers to the new commandment (*novum mandatum*) in John 13:34, appointed in the Prayer Book to be sung as an antiphon during the footwashing, which came to be called "the Maundy" in medieval England. The Proper Liturgy celebrates the events of the Last Supper, the footwashing and the institution of the eucharist. It is the only eucharist celebrated between Wednesday and the Great Vigil and ties the events of the Last Supper to those of Good Friday. It is appropriately celebrated as a Holy Week liturgy connecting the institution of the eucharist with the sacrifice of the cross.

The late medieval tradition of celebrating a festal eucharist in white vestments, with the singing of *Gloria in excelsis*, turning the day into a sort of Corpus Christi festival, was generally adopted by Anglicans in the late nineteenth and early twentieth centuries, but it has been widely rethought. It is possible to celebrate this as a festal eucharist, but the emphasis needs to be carried through consistently. Most places prefer a more subdued celebration, using the Holy Week red vestments and singing the *Trisagion* rather than the *Gloria in excelsis*. This helps to make the connection with the Good Friday liturgy.

The evening or late afternoon celebration of the eucharist on Maundy Thursday is mentioned by St. Augustine and was known to Egeria on her fourth-century visit to Jerusalem. Both spoke of the general reception of communion on the occasion. We have become accustomed to afternoon and evening celebrations of the eucharist, but for the Christians of late antiquity and the early Middle Ages the evening eucharist of Maundy Thursday was unique. Its very uniqueness tended to force the hour of celebration back into the morning, until the general revival of the evening eucharist in the twentieth century.

Two other events became associated with Maundy Thursday. One was the readmission of penitents to communion on this day, so that they could participate in the Easter eucharist. The custom in Rome is mentioned in a letter of Innocent I dating from 416, and a full rite for the purpose is found in the Gelasian Sacramentary of the seventh or eighth century. Although this rite was already obsolete by the eighth century, it underlies the choice of Maundy Thursday as a time for the Rite of Preparation for the Paschal Holy Days, with adults preparing for Reaffirmation of the Baptismal Covenant, in *The Book of Occasional Services*. The other event was the consecration of holy oils for use at the Easter baptisms on this day. The Gelasian Sacramentary contains a separate mass to be used for the blessing of the oils.

There is really no connection between Maundy Thursday and the blessing of oil. Chrism and the oil of the catechumens were needed for baptism at the Easter Vigil. The *Apostolic Tradition* expects the oils to be blessed at the vigil, immediately after the thanksgiving over the water (*Apostolic Tradition*, 6-8). This is the tradition adopted by *The Book of Common Prayer*, which expects the bishop to consecrate chrism when he or she administers baptism, immediately after giving thanks over the water (BCP 307).

The consecration of chrism has always been reserved to the bishop. In the East it is reserved to the patriarch or metropolitan, although the other oils may be blessed by presbyters. *The Book of Common Prayer* does not mention the use of oil of the catechumens. It follows the tradition in requiring the bishop to consecrate the chrism, but permitting the presbyter to bless the oil for the sick. The Western custom of blessing the oils at a special eucharist appears to have arisen in the fifth century. Maundy Thursday, the last eucharist before the Great Vigil, was the chosen day in Rome. In Spain, where distances were greater, the baptismal oils were blessed on Palm Sunday—apparently to allow more time for them to be delivered to the parishes where they would be used at the vigil. In some parts of northern Europe, this was done on the Fourth Sunday in Lent, allowing even more time for distribution.

The inclusion of the oil of the sick in the general blessing of oil appears to have been an afterthought. People brought their own oil to the church to be blessed, and took it home to administer to the sick afterwards.

1. The Chrism Mass

The tradition of a separate mass for the blessing of oils represented by the Gelasian *missa chrismalis* did not become normative in the Western church; rather, the oils were consecrated by the bishop at the ordinary Maundy Thursday eucharist at the cathedral. Those Anglican bishops who blessed holy oils generally followed this custom. In the 1951 Roman Catholic "restoration" of Holy Week rites, the chrism mass was revived. The *missa chrismatis* was a morning mass, with a new set of propers, in the course of which the oils were blessed. The epistle appointed was James 5:13-16 and the gospel Mark 6:7-13. Both refer to the anointing of the sick with oil.

Many Anglican dioceses have adopted, or have continued, the practice of having a special eucharist at the cathedral on Maundy Thursday, or some other convenient day in Holy Week, at which the oils are blessed. *The Book of Occasional Services* provides a form for the Consecration of Chrism Apart from Baptism and A Proper for the Consecration of Chrism, for use when "there is a need to consecrate Chrism at a separate, diocesan service" (BOS 234-236).

The lessons appointed for the rite in *The Book of Occasional Services* are substantially those in the new Roman Catholic rite: Isaiah 61:1-8 ("The spirit of the Lord God is upon me"), Revelation 1:4-8 ("and made us to be a kingdom of priests"), and Luke 4:16-21 (Jesus in the synagogue at Nazareth). Although there is a reference to Messianic anointing in Isaiah 61, which is repeated in Luke, the emphasis of the readings seems to be on ministry rather than anointing, especially when the Reaffirmation of Ordination Vows is a part of the service.

a. The Blessing of Oils

The liturgy itself can be very simply done, following the directions in *The Book of Occasional Services* (BOS 234-235). It may, of course be a sung liturgy with the usual ceremonial, but the blessing itself should not be unduly elaborated.

The olive oil is brought forward at the offertory in an ampulla large enough to be seen by the congregation. It is received by a deacon and placed on the credence table until after communion.

After the postcommunion prayer the ampulla is brought to the bishop, either at the altar or at a table placed in front of the altar where it can be more easily seen by the congregation. The deacon brings a small amount of aromatic oil, which the bishop adds to the chrism. This aromatic oil is traditionally called oil of balsam, but any fragrant oil may be used. Various oils are sold for the purpose as chrism essence.

The bishop says the short address to the congregation, places a hand on the ampulla of oil, and says or sings the consecration prayer, making the sign of the cross at "consecrate this oil." The liturgy concludes with the bishop's blessing and the dismissal.

b. The Reaffirmation of Ordination Vows

In the Roman Missal of Paul VI (1970) a new element was added to the chrism mass, the renewal of priestly vows. This became the dominant theme of a highly clericalized liturgy. In the words of the Anglican bishop Kenneth Stevenson:

> Those who like this new rite appreciate the opportunity of coming away from a busy parish at a busy time and reflecting together on the priesthood. Those who do not like this rite find it unnecessarily self-conscious, and may even see behind its introduction some of the internal disciplinary problems of the Roman Catholic Church's presbyterate in the late 1960s....Many Anglicans warm to this new service, while others suspect the renewal of priestly vows as being authoritarian in inspiration.[1]

In many Anglican dioceses the special eucharist held at the cathedral on Maundy Thursday for the blessing of oils has become the occasion for the renewal of ordination vows by the diocesan clergy, and a form for the purpose occurs in *The Book of Occasional Services*. Its rubrics include the statement:

> If the Renewal of Ordination Vows takes place on Maundy Thursday, it should be done at a celebration of the Eucharist other than the Proper Liturgy of the day. (BOS 237)

There is certainly nothing wrong with the renewal of ordination vows, even if one is suspicious of the historic origin of the Roman Catholic rite. Maundy Thursday, however, is not necessarily the best time to do this. Such a renewal might perhaps better follow the renewal of baptismal vows by the entire congregation at the Great Vigil, or some other baptismal feast. On Maundy Thursday it seems to separate the ordained from the rest of the baptized people of God and to suggest that the institution of the

---

1. Stevenson, *Jerusalem Revisited*, 43.

eucharist and the sacrifice of Christ are the particular concern of the ordained priesthood. Whether it is done or not, the inclusion of the renewal of vows in the chrismal eucharist requires greater consideration than it often receives.

c. Considerations of Time, Place, and Appropriateness

If the renewal of vows is not included, the chrism mass still raises a number of questions. There is no reason, except the convenience of the participants, to include the blessing of the oil for the sick. *The Book of Common Prayer* clearly permits individual presbyters to bless the oil prior to its use. If it is desired to have the bishop bless healing oil for the diocese, it could be more appropriately done at a diocesan healing service celebrated by the bishop at the cathedral, the diocesan hospital, or some other suitable place. St. Luke's feast day suggests itself as an appropriate time. The Mozarabic liturgy had such a celebration on the feast of the holy physicians Cosmas and Damian.

The Prayer Book, of course, expects the chrism to be consecrated at the bishop's visitation of individual parishes (BCP 307) "for use by a priest at baptisms in that parish which take place on subsequent occasions in the year" (BOS 228). Chrism is the aromatic olive oil traditionally used at baptism. It is a symbol of the anointing of Christ with the Holy Spirit at his baptism, and is used to mark the cross on the foreheads of the newly baptized, who are Christ's own forever. The anointing with chrism was seen by writers of the early church as identifying the Christian with Christ, the anointed one. Its use was restored to the baptismal rite in the 1979 *Book of Common Prayer*. It is *baptismal* oil; although it has been used by Roman Catholics at confirmation and ordinations, the Prayer Book does not follow that tradition, and there is no reason to anoint again those who have been signed with the chrism in baptism.

The form in *The Book of Occasional Services* for Consecration of Chrism Apart from Baptism "is intended for use when, because of the absence of candidates for Baptism, the consecration of Chrism takes place at the time of Confirmation" (BOS 234-235), as provided in the Prayer Book by a rubric on page 419. It is the Proper for the Consecration of Chrism which mentions "a separate, diocesan service" (BOS 236), and the Reaffirmation of Ordination Vows which mentions Maundy Thursday.

The practice recommended by *The Book of Common Prayer* is preferable to a separate, diocesan service. It is certainly preferable to a clericalized diocesan service on a work-day morning, which suggests that the consecration of chrism is the concern only of clergy. There may, nevertheless, be good pastoral reasons to hold such a diocesan service. Even the appointed readings from *The Book of Occasional Services*, when not followed by the renewal of ordination vows, can be interpreted in a Messianic sense to refer to the baptismal ministry of the whole people of God as a royal priesthood. There is, of course, a long-standing Western tradition for doing this on Maundy Thursday, but it can just as easily be done on a more convenient day and at a time when lay people can also participate.

2. Maundy Thursday Rite of Preparation for the Paschal Holy Days

This rite from *The Book of Occasional Services* (BOS 144-145) is intended to be used with baptized persons who have been preparing for reaffirmation of the Baptismal Covenant at the Easter Vigil and with their sponsors. It is one of the rites, parallel to the catechumenate, for those already baptized which were prepared in response to the call of the 1988 General Convention, and is an adaptation of the ancient rite for the Solemn Reconciliation of Penitents on this day. The rite takes place in the context of the Proper Liturgy of Maundy Thursday, not at a separate service.

Before the footwashing, the candidates and their sponsors come forward. The presider addresses them, inviting them to participate in the footwashing, both by having their own feet washed and by washing the feet of others. The candidates respond, "We are prepared." The presider addresses them, using the invitation to confession from Form Two of the Reconciliation of Penitents, "Now, in the presence of Christ..." (BCP 450). The candidates kneel and say together the confession of sin, omitting the mention of specific sins by leaving out the passage "Especially, I confess...and all other sins I cannot now remember," and continuing, "I turn to you in sorrow...." The priest lays a hand in turn on the head of each candidate, saying the first form of absolution: "Our Lord Jesus Christ, who offered himself...." The candidates sit, and the presider then washes their feet. If there are many candidates, other ministers may assist in the footwashing. The presider then distributes basins, towels, and pitchers of water to the candidates, saying to each, "May Christ strengthen you in the service he lays upon you." The candidates wash the feet of other members of the congregation.

Following the footwashing the liturgy continues with the Peace. Eucharistic Prayer D may be used and intercessions for the church and the world included in it.

3. The Proper Liturgy

The Proper Liturgy of Maundy Thursday commemorating the Last Supper is an evening celebration. A Lenten off-white or special Holy Week frontal remains on the altar. Red vestments are worn. Additional priests and deacons who participate in the liturgy may wear alb and red stole. It is fitting for other priests attached to the congregation to stand near the altar and join with the presider in the eucharist, and for all parish deacons to take part. Additional priests may serve as ministers of the footwashing and of communion, but they may not usurp the deacons' functions or inhibit the participation of lay people in the rite. The distinctive elements of the liturgy are the washing of feet, the reservation of the Sacrament for Good Friday communion, and the stripping of the altar.

The reservation of the Sacrament is for the purpose of administering communion at the Good Friday liturgy. If communion is not to be administered on Good Friday, then the Sacrament is consumed following the reception of communion at this liturgy.

> When the Sacrament is to be reserved for administration on Good Friday, it should be kept in a separate chapel or other place apart from the main sanctuary of the church, in order that on Good Friday the attention of the congregation may be on the bare main Altar. (BOS 94)

In many places the Sacrament is reserved in a place where people may keep watch before it, following the example of the apostles whom Jesus asked to watch and pray with him after the Last Supper (Matthew 26:40-41). This all-night vigil apparently began, like so many other Holy Week ceremonies, in fourth-century Jerusalem. It is, however, by no means necessary to have a watch in a Garden of Repose in order to celebrate the Proper Liturgies of Maundy Thursday and Good Friday. The Sacrament may be taken simply to a chapel or to the sacristy and kept there until the communion on Good Friday. An alternative form of the watch is to keep vigil in the empty church before the bare altar.

There are two partially inconsistent explanations of the ceremony of washing feet. One is that it is a dramatic portrayal of the actions of Jesus at the Last Supper. The presider washes the feet of twelve men to imitate what Christ did. This view is implied in the introductory address included in *The Book of Occasional Services* (BOS 93), which describes the footwashing as "an act of humble service" of which the ordained clergy need particularly to be reminded. The priest invites the representatives of the congregation to come forward "that I may recall whose servant I am by following the example of my Master." This was certainly the medieval understanding of the footwashing. The congregation saw the bishop, or abbot, or (in England) the king wash the feet of twelve ordinary folk and were reminded that even the highest were servants of the servants of God.

The second explanation focuses on two passages from John's gospel: the new commandment and the command which concludes the Maundy gospel.

> I give you a new commandment, that you love one another. Just as I have loved you, you also should love one another. (John 13:34)

> So if I, your Lord and Teacher, have washed your feet, you ought also to wash one another's feet. For I have set you an example, that you also should do as I have done to you. (John 13:14-15)

In this explanation the washing of feet is the outward and visible sign of the love of Christ, which we are commanded to share with one another. We therefore wash one another's feet as Christ commanded that we all may share in that love. It is not an acted parable to be watched, but an action in which all are invited to participate. This version lacks the hierarchic assumptions of the first explanation, and clearly underlies the Maundy Thursday Rite of Preparation for the Paschal Holy Days in *The Book of Occasional Services*. Yet there is truth in both perceptions. We are called to both love and humility. The second explanation causes congregations to wish for a more general sharing of the sign of footwashing, which requires careful planning, lest the entire process dissolve into chaos.

4. The Liturgy in Detail

a. The Entrance and Lessons

The eucharist begins in the usual manner. The *Trisagion* is sung. All three lessons are read. The Johannine gospel of the footwashing is the traditional gospel for the day, and if the footwashing will take place, it is always used. If the footwashing is not to be performed, the Luke passage may be used. The reading from 1 Corinthians narrates the institution of the eucharist.

The footwashing follows the gospel and homily. If the Maundy Thursday Rite of Preparation for the Paschal Holy Days is to be used, it precedes the footwashing, and the introduction to the footwashing in *The Book of Occasional Services* is omitted.

b. The Footwashing

If there is to be a general invitation to all to participate in the footwashing, instruction needs to be given ahead of time about what to wear for the service. People need to be told to wear easily removable shoes and socks, and those who are unprepared or who do not wish to participate must not be made to feel excluded or embarrassed. Sufficient ministers to begin the washing need to be recruited. Church wardens, members of the vestry, and other parish leaders are appropriate choices. Chairs or benches for those whose feet will be washed are placed at the front of the nave, or in the chancel, before the service. Basins, towels, and pitchers of water are placed nearby, or brought in at the beginning of the rite.

The presider removes the chasuble and the deacon(s) the dalmatic before washing feet, following the example of Jesus. The additional ministers of the footwashing come forward and take their places. If they have been seated in the congregation they do not vest. Aprons may be provided for the footwashers. The presider stands before the congregation and invites them to come forward to participate in the footwashing. If a less hierarchical explanation of the ceremony is desired, the introduction in *The Book of Occasional Services* may be amended along these lines:

> Fellow servants of our Lord Jesus Christ: On the night before his death, Jesus set an example for his disciples by washing their feet, an act of humble service. He taught that strength and growth in the kingdom of God come not by power, authority, or even miracle, but by such lowly service, and he commanded them to follow his example by washing one another's feet.
>
> Therefore I invite you [who have been appointed as representatives of the congregation and] who share in the royal priest-

hood of Christ to come forward, that we may follow the example of our Master, remembering the new commandment that he gave this night, "Love one another as I have loved you. By this shall the world know that you are my disciples: That you have love for one another."

It must be made clear to the congregation whether only designated representatives will have their feet washed, or whether everyone in the congregation is welcome to come forward. They also need to understand whether they are only to have their feet washed, or whether they are invited to wash the feet of others. The larger the congregation the more important it is for everyone involved to be clear about what they are doing. If everyone is invited to come forward, it is still a good idea to designate certain people to begin the process, and if others are invited to join in the footwashing some people should be prepared to wash the feet of the original group of ministers after they have had their own feet washed. If the group is large, sacristans or altar guild members need to be ready with more water, clean towels, and empty basins. The washers pour water over one bare foot of each person, dry it with the towel, and then do the same with the other foot.

During the footwashing, the anthems appointed in the Prayer Book, or other suitable anthems, are sung. Music for the anthems may be found at S 344–S 347 in the Appendix to the Accompaniment Edition of *The Hymnal 1982*. Appropriate hymns include versions of *Ubi caritas* (Hymns 576/577, 606) and the Ghanian folk song "Jesu, Jesu" (Hymn 602). The Taizé chant *Ubi caritas*, which can be sung by the congregation while moving about during the footwashing, is another possibility.

After the footwashing the presider and deacon(s) resume their outer vestments, the other washers return to their places, the basins, water, and towels are removed, and the service continues with the Prayers of the People.

c. The Holy Communion

If communion is to be offered on Good Friday, an additional flagon or flagons large enough to hold wine for all expected to communicate on Good Friday and additional bread with an appropriate container (plate or ciborium) are brought forward at the offertory, along with the provisions for this service. Eucharistic Prayer A with the Holy Week preface, or Eucharistic Prayer D are appropriate.

After communion the consecrated bread and wine not being reserved for Good Friday communion are consumed. Any reserved Sacrament is also consumed at this time and the aumbry or tabernacle left open. The consecrated bread and wine for the Good Friday communion are left on the altar. If the consecrated bread is on a plate or paten it may be covered by a linen cloth. After the Holy Week Prayer over the People (BOS 26), the Sacrament is taken to the place of reservation as directly as possible; a solemn procession carrying the Sacrament around the church is inappropriate. Traditionally the hymn "Now, my tongue, the mystery telling" accompanies this action, and may be sung kneeling. The presider may cense the Sacrament. The presider takes the consecrated bread and goes to the place of reservation. A deacon, or an assisting priest, carries the flagon. The torchbearers may carry the altar candles before them and leave the candles in the place of reservation. They leave the Sacrament and return to the church for the stripping of the altar. The dismissal is omitted.

If the Sacrament is not to be reserved, the stripping directly follows the Prayer over the People.

d. The Stripping of the Altar

The stripping of the altar removes the ornaments of the sanctuary, leaving it bare and empty for the Good Friday liturgy. The presider removes the chasuble and stole and the deacon(s) the dalmatic and stole. Altar hangings and other moveable ornaments are removed to the sacristy. All remaining candles are extinguished and removed and the lights in the sanctuary are turned out. This may be done in silence, or Psalm 22 may be recited (without the *Gloria Patri*). It may be recited in unison by the congregation, antiphonally between men and women, sides of the church, or choir and congregation. The antiphon which follows may be recited by all before and after the psalm: "They divide my garments among them; they cast lots for my clothing" (BOS 94). There is no dismissal. The congregation leave in silence, or remain to keep watch.

5. A Maundy Thursday *Agapé*

The celebration of a *Seder,* either in its proper Jewish form or in a Christian adaptation, is inappropriate on Maundy Thursday. Easter (not Maundy Thursday) is the Christian Passover, and festal meals in general are not appropriate during Holy Week.

The *agapé* (or "love-feast") was a regular feature of the life of the early church, as attested by writers from Ignatius of Antioch to Augustine of Hippo. Apparently when the celebration of the eucharist was separated from an actual meal, the tradition of fellowship meals modeled on the Lord's Supper remained. The bishop or other minister blessed the food. The *agapé* eventually became a sort of charity supper in which the church fed the poor, but its original purpose was Christian table fellowship.

The Book of Occasional Services contains an order for a simple meal to be shared after the Maundy Thursday eucharist, recalling the meal Jesus and his disciples shared in the upper room, with blessings over the wine, bread, and other foods (BOS 95-96). It suggests that the *agapé* follow the eucharist, and precede the stripping of the altar. It may, nevertheless, be more practical to conclude the liturgy with the stripping of the altar as described above and to hold the *agapé* afterward for those able to remain.

6. Maundy Thursday in Small Congregations

Any congregation which has a Sunday eucharist can celebrate the Maundy Thursday liturgy. It should be held in the evening, or whenever the majority of the congregation are able to attend. Often the scheduling of a simple meal after the service (see the previous section) will make it easier for working people to attend. The church is prepared for the eucharist, with Holy Week red vestments, and, unless the church has a special Holy Week frontal, the Lenten frontal may remain on the altar, if the color does not clash with the vestments.

If the washing of feet is to be a part of the service, seats at the front of the congregation for those whose feet are being washed and sufficient basins, towels, and pitchers of water will be needed. Members of the vestry or other parish leaders may be recruited as ministers of the footwashing. A decision must be made as to whether a representative group of people will have their feet washed, or a general invitation will be issued to the congregation to have their feet washed and to join in the washing of the feet of others. Those whose feet will be washed need to be reminded to wear easily removable shoes and socks.

If communion is to be administered from the reserved Sacrament on Good Friday, then an extra paten of bread and flagon or cruet of wine must be prepared and brought forward at the offertory. The Sacrament should not be reserved in the church lest it distract people during the Good Friday liturgy. It may be reserved in the sacristy, or in a chapel or place set apart where people may watch and pray.

The eucharist begins in the usual manner of a Sunday eucharist. The *Trisagion* or *Kyrie* is sung. Lay persons read the lessons. The psalm is recited or sung to a simple chant. The deacon (or presider if there is no deacon) reads the gospel in the same way it is done at the Sunday liturgy. If the Maundy Thursday Rite of Preparation for the Paschal Holy Days is to be used, it follows the sermon.

After the sermon, the presider removes the chasuble, comes to the center of the sanctuary, and invites the people to come forward to have their feet washed. The other ministers of the footwashing come forward and stand beside the presider. The invitation in *The Book of Occasional Services* may be altered as indicated in the previous section to make it less clerical. If there are many people whose feet will be washed, servers or altar guild members must be ready to provide clean towels, fill pitchers with water, and empty basins. The washers pour water over the bare foot of each person, dry it with the towel, and then do the same with the other foot.

The anthems in *The Book of Common Prayer* may be sung or recited, or hymns may be sung during the footwashing. Hymn 576/577 ("God is love") and Hymn 602 ("Jesu, Jesu, fill us with you love") are particularly appropriate. After the footwashing all return to their places, the presider puts the chasuble on, the utensils are taken to the sacristy, and the liturgy continues with the Prayers of the People.

If the Sacrament is to be reserved, the additional consecrated bread and wine are left on the altar after communion. The rest of the elements are consumed, and if the Sacrament is regularly reserved in the church, the reserved Sacrament is consumed as well and the tabernacle or aumbry left open. A portable communion set may be prepared and kept in case of an emergency sick communion between the Maundy Thursday liturgy and the Great Vigil.

The presider says the postcommunion prayer and the Holy Week Prayer over the People. Everyone then kneels and the hymn "Now, my tongue, the mystery telling" is sung. During the hymn the presider or deacon takes the sacrament to the place of reservation without any special ceremony. The servers may remove the altar candles and carry them with the sacrament, leaving them there. The presider removes the chasuble and stole, returns to the church, and presides over the stripping of the altar. This may be done in silence, or Psalm 22 may be read with this antiphon: "They divide my garments among them; they cast lots for my clothing" (BOS 94). The servers and altar guild members remove the altar frontal and other ornaments in the sanctuary. There is no blessing or dismissal. Everyone leaves in silence, leaving the altar bare.

Chapter Seven

Good Friday

The observance of the Friday before Easter as a commemoration of the crucifixion can be traced back to Jerusalem in the fourth century. Prior to that time Easter had been a unitive celebration of the passion and resurrection. The *Pascha* combined both fast and feast and included the entire saving event of Christ's dying and rising again: crucifixion and resurrection were celebrated as a single event in its many aspects, as God's victory in Christ over sin and death. It was not until the fourth century, when the observance of Good Friday spread throughout the Christian East and then to the West, that the two aspects were separated into Good Friday and Easter celebrations. The Good Friday proper liturgy consists of three parts: the Liturgy of the Word, the veneration of the cross, and communion from the reserved Sacrament. The celebration of the eucharist on Good Friday was already forbidden in 416, when Innocent I mentioned it in a letter to Decentius, Bishop of Gubbio. The American *Book of Common Prayer* has maintained this tradition.

The Good Friday Liturgy of the Word was the ancient form of liturgy used on aliturgical days—that is, on days on which the eucharist was not celebrated. At one time this would have included all fast days, and therefore all of the weekdays of Lent, except the Annunciation. This is still the Byzantine tradition.

The Good Friday Word liturgy lacks an entrance rite and begins immediately with the collect and readings. The old Roman rite lacked even an opening collect, but began with the silent entry of the ministers, who prostrated themselves before the altar, and moved immediately to an Old Testament reading, Hosea 6:1-6. In Rome St. John's Passion was the gospel assigned to the Friday before Easter, because Wednesday and Friday were the station days on which the Liturgy of the Word was regularly celebrated. St. Matthew's Passion was assigned to the preceding Sunday and Mark and John to the station days during the week, Wednesday and Friday respectively.

The solemn collects, a striking feature of the Good Friday liturgy, are the old Roman form of the Prayers of the People. They are a trialogue, in which the deacon bids the people to silent prayer, the people pray, and the presiding bishop or priest concludes the silent prayer with a collect, collecting the prayers offered by the people. On Sundays this was done with everyone standing, but on fast days the deacon bade everyone kneel to pray and then to stand for the presider's collect.

The Word liturgy is followed by the veneration of the cross. This is a ceremony brought home by pilgrims from Jerusalem, where, as the fourth-century pilgrim Egeria tells us, the true cross was displayed at what was believed to be the actual site of the crucifixion for the faithful to venerate. Pilgrims brought home not only the ceremony, but relics of the cross as well. St. Helena, the Emperor Constantine's mother, brought a piece of the cross to Rome, where it was placed in the Basilica of the Holy Cross in Jerusalem built for the purpose. In the eighth century the pope led a procession to this church on Good Friday for the veneration of the cross. The popularity of the ceremony caused a shift from the use of a relic to the use of any wooden cross available for the purpose.

The final part of the Good Friday liturgy, communion from the reserved Sacrament, was the regular Byzantine custom on fast days. On these days there was no celebration of the eucharist, but at the end of the evening office, in what was called the Liturgy of the Presanctified Gifts, communion was distributed to the people from the reserved Sacrament. It became a part of the Good Friday liturgy at Rome in the eighth century, but it never became a part of the Ambrosian or Mozarabic liturgies.

The Book of Common Prayer (1979) includes all three parts of this rite in its Good Friday liturgy, although the veneration of the cross and communion are both optional.

Earlier versions of the Prayer Book in England and America did not contain any special liturgical provisions for Good Friday. Proper lessons for the offices and a collect, epistle, and gospel, with no instruction as to how they were to be used, were included. Many congregations conducted one or both offices and the ante-communion, or Word liturgy. In the nineteenth century some Evangelical parishes celebrated the eucharist on Good Friday, and the Canadian *Book of Alternative Services* and the English *Lent, Holy Week, Easter* permit this as an alternative to communion from the reserved Sacrament (BAS 317, LHWE 196-197), but the devotional thrust of the day has often been a nonliturgical service of preaching on the seven last words of Christ. Called the Three Hours, this service is conducted from noon to three o'clock, and is based on a Latin American Jesuit service. The offices and the Word liturgy did not provide a sufficiently rigorous spiritual diet for most people on this day.

Massey Shepherd, in his 1958 *Holy Week Offices,* included the solemn collects and the veneration of the cross for use with the ante-communion, and suggested a number of possible schedules for the liturgical observance of Good Friday. An Anglican adaptation of the Roman Catholic Mass of the Presanctified was included in both editions of the Cowley *Holy Week Manual* and in *The American Missal, The Anglican Missal,* and *The American Missal Revised.* None of these were "authorized," but they were used in some places. In 1970, *Prayer Book Studies 19* for the first time officially suggested the possibility of administering communion from the reserved Sacrament at the conclusion of the Good Friday liturgy.

For many, it is difficult to imagine doing the Good Friday liturgy without the veneration of the cross, although *The Book of Common Prayer* clearly permits it. The veneration of the cross, following the intercessory solemn collects, occupies the same space in the liturgy taken on other occasions by the offertory and the Great Thanksgiving; devotion before the cross thus fulfills a quasi-sacramental function on Good Friday, forming a logical focus of the rite, and one to which the piety of the people can respond. In the Middle Ages the veneration was called "creeping to the cross," and people approached the cross on their knees, making three genuflections and kissing the wood or the feet of the figure of Christ. Today cultural diversity has produced a variety of expressions. Some congregations prefer the full ceremony, with kissing, weeping, and genuflections. Others prefer to kneel in the pews looking at the cross, meditating and singing a hymn. Still others choose something in between. Ending the liturgy with the veneration produces a complete liturgy in accord with both tradition and contemporary piety.

Addressing the issue of whether communion should be administered on Good Friday, the Church of England's *Lent, Holy Week, Easter* comments:

> It would seem that on this above all other days, it is wholly appropriate to eat the bread and drink the cup, thereby proclaiming the Lord's death until he comes.... It is the sacramental means whereby the believer, together with the whole Church, is drawn into the movement of Christ's own self-offering to the Father, that full, perfect, and sufficient sacrifice, oblation, and satisfaction for the sins of the whole world, made once and for all by the Saviour's death upon the cross. (LHWE 197)

Among Lutherans and Anglican Evangelicals this belief has often resulted in the celebration of the eucharist on Good Friday, and this custom, although forbidden by the American Prayer Book, is permitted by both the Church of England and the Anglican Church of Canada. The objections to it are first that it is contrary to long-standing Christian tradition in both East and West, second that it seems to make the eucharist too narrowly a commemoration of the crucifixion, excluding the resurrection and the other aspects of Christ's redeeming work, and third that the inherently festal nature of the eucharist is inconsistent with the observance of Good Friday as a solemn fast. Certainly the piety of those groups which have celebrated the eucharist on Good Friday has often viewed the eucharist more as a penitential rite than as a celebration. The ministration of communion from the reserved Sacrament appears to meet the objections while keeping the positive values of receiving communion on this day so well expressed in the passage quoted above from *Lent, Holy Week, Easter*.

Communion from the reserved Sacrament as a part of a public liturgy, in turn, raises questions for others, since this has never been a part of the tradition of the Anglican Church until recently. The real argument, however, is not over theology but piety. Receiving communion on Good Friday is an important element in the observance of and participation in the mighty acts celebrated in the liturgy on this day for many people, and when the ministration of communion is omitted they feel deprived and their sense of participation is reduced. For many others, however, the receiving of communion is no part of their Good Friday piety. They receive at the Maundy Thursday eucharist and at the Great Vigil of Easter, while Good Friday is a day to focus on the cross, and its liturgy is tied to the eucharist of the previous evening. Both sides can claim a long tradition of support for their position, and *The Book of Common Prayer* clearly permits either option. Neither can claim that the church has "always done it this way." The tradition has been different in different places, and it still is. We shall include the ministration of communion in our description of the Good Friday liturgy but need to emphasize its optional nature.

The Good Friday liturgy is a solemn commemoration of and participation in the great events of this day, the salvation of the human race through the victory of Christ, who by dying destroyed death, not a funeral for Jesus. Its theme is well-expressed in the first anthem for the veneration of the cross:

We glory in your cross, O Lord,
    and praise and glorify your holy resurrection;

for by virtue of your cross

joy has come to the whole world. (BCP 281)

The older custom of wearing black vestments, and the Anglican custom in some places of vesting choir and acolytes in black cassocks without surplices on this day, tends to reinforce the funereal theme. This latter custom apparently stems from the recognition that the Three Hours was not a liturgical service, and hence "vestments" were not worn, but only the cassock, the "street dress" of the clergy. The liturgical color today is Holy Week red, for Christ the King of martyrs, and albs or surplices are appropriately worn.

The liturgy may be celebrated at any convenient hour at which the majority of the congregation can participate. In some places the liturgy is celebrated at noon, in others it will take place in the evening.

1. The Good Friday Liturgy

The Good Friday liturgy is celebrated in a bare church. Crosses have either been veiled or removed. No altar frontal or other ornament is used. The clergy wear alb and Holy Week red stoles. The presider may wear a cope or chasuble. If communion is to be distributed, the corporal, chalice, and other vessels are placed on the credence table.

a. The Collect and Lessons

The ministers enter in silence, without processional cross or candles. All bow to the altar and kneel is silence, or they may prostrate themselves before the altar. After a period of silent prayer (traditionally long enough to say the *Miserere*, Psalm 51), all rise and go to their places.

The presider faces the congregation and says or sings, "Blessed be our God" (Hymnal Appendix S 348, Accompaniment Edition Volume 1) and the Good Friday collect. All sit for the readings and psalm.

St. John's Passion is read or sung as on Palm Sunday: the same alternatives are available, though it is not necessary to make the same choices. None of the readers of the passion gospel need be ordained. A passion hymn or silence is appropriate between the epistle and the passion. It is preferable to use the longer form of the passion gospel to include more of the narrative.

Following the passion gospel the sermon is preached and a hymn may be sung (BCP 277).

b. The Solemn Collects

The deacon goes to the center of the sanctuary facing the people, or to the lectern, and begins the introduction to the solemn collects. The biddings may be spoken or sung to the music in *The Altar Book*. The indented portions of the biddings may be omitted or adapted as appropriate (BCP 277). At the conclusion of each bidding, the deacon may say (or sing): "Let us kneel in silent prayer." All kneel in place. The deacon says (or sings), "Arise," and stands up. All stand, and the presider says or sings the collect.

Alternatively, the kneeling and rising may be omitted and the congregation either stand or kneel for all the petitions and collects. If they are to kneel, the deacon may say, "Let us kneel" before the "Let us pray..." of the first petition. If the congregation remains kneeling throughout, the deacon and presider do not kneel.

The service may conclude after the solemn collects with a hymn, the Lord's Prayer, and the final prayer (BCP 280), but this is not recommended.

c. The Veneration of the Cross

A wooden cross or crucifix large enough to be clearly visible throughout the church is brought into the church. Whether a cross or crucifix is used is largely a matter of taste, availability, and cultural preference. The important thing is that it be large enough and suitable to be the focus of the congregation's devotion. In some congregations a rough-hewn wooden cross, carrying overtones of the old rugged cross, is best, while in others nothing but a realistic crucifix will do. A deacon, or some other person, lay or ordained, enters the church from the narthex or gathering space carrying the cross. If the cross is very large, it may be necessary for two people to carry it. Torchbearers carrying lighted candles walk on either side of the cross. During the procession Anthem 1, "We glory in your cross, O Lord" (BCP 288; Hymnal Appendix, S 349), or one of the other anthems in the Prayer Book may be sung, or the entry may take place in silence. The cross is placed in a stand in front of the altar, and the torches on either side of it. If the cross is placed in front of the altar, it is placed so as not to block the use of the altar to distribute communion. If this is impossible, or if it must be placed on the altar, the acolyte moves it at the conclusion of the veneration.

An alternative method of bringing in the cross is to make three stations while processing down the aisle from the church door. These are made in the same places as the stations with the paschal candle at the Great Vigil. The person carrying the cross stops and faces the congregation, displaying the cross, and says or sings, "This is the wood of the cross, on which hung the Savior of the world," to which all reply, "Come, let us worship." These words are repeated at each station with the versicle and response at a higher pitch. This is the form of the procession in the *Lutheran Book of Worship* and one of two forms in the Roman Sacramentary. The text of the versicle and response, originally the antiphon on Psalm 119 sung in Rome during the procession to the Church of Holy Cross, is that found in the Roman Sacramentary and the Canadian *Book of Alternative Services* (BAS 313). Some congregations may wish to have a more extensive procession, with the people joining in behind the cross, going around the church or (in suitable climates) outdoors. They might even follow the Way of the Cross if an extended procession were desired.

Three anthems to be sung during the veneration are in *The Book of Common Prayer*, with music in the Appendix to *The Hymnal 1982* (S 349–S 351). The Prayer Book also permits "other suitable anthems" to be sung. *The Draft Proposed Book of Common Prayer* of 1976 included between

Anthem 1 and Anthem 2 the text of the Reproaches, sung since the Middle Ages during the veneration. They are an extended meditation on the theme from Micah, "O my people, what have I done unto thee, or wherein have I wearied thee? Testify against me!" (Micah 6:3). The General Convention omitted this text from *The Book of Common Prayer* because some felt that it would be interpreted as anti-Semitic by identifying "my people," whose responsibility for Christ's death is acknowledged, with the Jews. The rubric clearly permits the use of the Reproaches, however, and this fact was noted when the text was dropped. In 1979 a revised version of the Reproaches was published in *Ashes to Fire* and the text was subsequently included in the Canadian *Book of Alternative Services* (BAS 314-316). This text is not as susceptible to an anti-Semitic interpretation because it clearly identifies "my people" with the church. The response used throughout in this version is the *Trisagion*, which can be sung to any of the many available chants. All, or any combination of the anthems and the Reproaches, may be used.

The traditional form of the veneration was for the ministers and people to come forward, making three genuflections as they approached the cross, and then to kiss the foot of the cross. This is substantially modified in most places. The simplest form is for everyone to kneel facing the cross while the anthems are sung. The presider and deacon, or all of the liturgical ministers, may come to the center and kneel before the cross. Opportunity may be given for individuals to come forward and kneel before the cross, but a more corporate approach is for all to kneel looking at the cross during the anthems.

The hymn "Sing, my tongue, the glorious battle" (Hymn 165/166), or some other hymn extolling the glory of the cross, is then sung (BCP 282). The music for this hymn arranged with the verse "Faithful cross! above all other" as a refrain is found at S 352 in the Appendix. The hymn concludes the veneration.

If Holy Communion is not to be administered, the liturgy ends with the Lord's Prayer and the final prayer on page 282 of the Prayer Book.

d. *Communion from the Reserved Sacrament*

During the hymn the deacon, standing behind the altar, spreads the corporal on the center of the altar and arranges the vessels for the reception of communion. When all is ready the deacon, accompanied by another minister if more than one person is needed to carry the Sacrament, goes to the place of reservation and returns with the sacrament. If there is no deacon, this is done by an assisting priest. If there are no assisting clergy, the presider prepares the table and fetches the Sacrament. This may be done during the hymn or in silence after the hymn. If the altar candles were not put in place for the veneration of the cross, they are brought in by the torchbearers with the Sacrament and set in their usual places on the altar.

The deacon goes behind the altar to the center and places the Sacrament on the corporal, divides the bread (if there will be more than one bread minister) among the necessary number of patens or plates, and fills the chalices from the flagon. If there are two deacons, they do this together. The deacon returns to the presider's right. A second deacon goes to the left.

The deacon says the invitation to the Confession of Sin, facing the people. The deacon and presider bow low or kneel, facing the altar, during the confession. The presider, standing and facing the people, says the absolution. The presider and deacon reverence the altar and take their customary places behind it. The acolyte brings *The Altar Book* with its cushion or stand to the altar and places it to the priest's left.

The presider says or sings the introduction to the Lord's Prayer and joins the people in saying or singing it. If additional ministers of communion are needed, they now come to the altar. The presider and deacon raise the elements in the usual way and the presider says, "The gifts of God for the people of God." Communion is administered in the usual manner. A hymn, psalm, or anthem may be sung during communion, or the action may take place in silence.

After communion all the remaining consecrated bread and wine are consumed; if it has not already been done, a small portion may be reserved for emergency sick communions. As these should be reserved in a portable communion set and kept in the sacristy or some other suitable place, this

---

is most conveniently done before the Sacrament is brought into the church. The vessels are cleansed in the customary way and returned to the credence table or to the sacristy. The corporal is folded up and removed. The presider, standing at the altar or at the chair, says or sings the final prayer. There is no blessing or dismissal. The torchbearers may carry the altar candles with them to the sacristy, or the candles may be extinguished and removed after the service. The ministers leave in silence and return to the sacristy. Any ornaments remaining in the sanctuary are removed.

2. Other Good Friday Services

The Good Friday liturgy is celebrated only once. Other possible services are Morning Prayer (if the liturgy is celebrated in the afternoon or evening) or Evensong (if the liturgy is celebrated in the morning or at noon). The Way of the Cross (described above in the Lent section) is a particularly appropriate service for Good Friday, and may be held at any hour when another service seems desirable. It is also adaptable as a children's service.

The preaching service known as the Three Hours was once the most popular Good Friday service, and it some places it is still well-attended. It is often held as an ecumenical service, or as a joint service of nearby congregations, with clergy of various churches sharing the preaching. Less frequently a single preacher undertakes to preach all of the sermons. If this service is held from noon to three o'clock, the Good Friday liturgy will either be held in the evening or mid-morning. A large church in a business district may find all of these possibilities desirable, but most parishes will need to focus on the Good Friday liturgy and perhaps one other service. None of the other services should usurp the place of the Proper Liturgy of the Day.

3. Good Friday in Small Congregations

A small congregation can do the Good Friday liturgy simply and well. If the congregation has good musical resources, it may use some of the more ambitious musical items. If it has few, the anthems may be read responsively. If communion is to be distributed, the corporal, chalice, and any other vessels needed are placed on the credence table. The altar is bare, without frontal, altar cloths, or candles. The presider and deacon wear albs and red stoles, and the presider may wear a cope or chasuble.

The procession enters in silence, without processional cross or torches. All kneel or prostrate themselves before the altar in silent prayer. The presider stands, faces the people, and says (or sings) the acclamation "Blessed be our God," and the Good Friday collect. The presider sits, and a reader begins the first reading. The psalm may be read responsively or sung to a simplified Anglican chant or other congregational chant. A reader reads the lesson from Hebrews. A passion hymn may be sung, or silence may be kept before the reading of the passion gospel. The passion is read with lay persons from the congregation taking the different parts, as on Palm Sunday. The congregation may read the part of the crowd, for which they require texts. The narrator (the deacon or a lay person) goes to the pulpit or lectern; the other readers stand where they can be seen and heard. The presider may read the words of Jesus, or another reader may do so. The congregation may sit until the mention of the arrival at Golgotha, when all stand (BCP 277). It is desirable that the longer text of the passion be used. The sermon follows the passion.

The biddings to the solemn collects may be read by the deacon or a lay person, with the presider saying the collects. The reader stands at the lectern and faces the congregation for the biddings. The presider stands at the chair. The people may stand throughout, or the reader may direct them to kneel after the introduction to the biddings, "We pray, therefore, for people everywhere according to their needs." Alternatively, the reader may say, "Let us kneel in silent prayer" at the end of each bidding and "Arise" before the collect. In this case the reader and presider kneel and stand with the people. The biddings may be adapted as indicated in *The Book of Common Prayer* (BCP 277).

After the solemn collects, a wooden cross or crucifix is brought into the church. It is carried from the church door to the sanctuary, where it is set up in a stand to be the focus of the devotions which follow. If the church is very small, it may be necessary to use a smaller cross and place it on the altar. The deacon, a server, or a member of the congregation designated by the presider carries the cross. Servers may carry candles or processional torches on either side of the cross, and place them on either side of the cross on the sanctuary floor or on the altar. If the alternative form of the procession and veneration is desired, the directions above on the veneration of the cross may be followed. The entry of the cross may take place in silence or the presider and congregation may recite Anthem 1 from the Prayer Book (BCP 281) responsively, or the anthem may be sung. All kneel facing the cross and recite the remaining anthems responsively with the presider, or the choir may sing them. The revised version of the Reproaches from the Canadian *Book of Alternative Services* may be said with everyone singing the *Trisagion* to one of the tunes in *The Hymnal 1982* as a response. The veneration concludes with the singing of the hymn "Sing, my tongue, the glorious battle."

If communion is not to be distributed, the presider stands at the conclusion of the hymn and introduces the Lord's Prayer. All say the Lord's Prayer and the presider says the closing prayer. All leave in silence.

If communion is to be distributed, the deacon (or the presider) spreads the corporal and places the chalice and any other necessary vessels on the altar. The acolyte brings *The Altar Book* to the altar and places it to the left of the priest. The deacon (or the presider) goes to the place of reservation and brings the Sacrament to the altar, placing the bread on the paten and the wine in the chalice. This may be done during the hymn, or silently after the hymn. The deacon (or the presider), standing at the altar or at the chair, faces the people and says the invitation to the Confession of Sin. The deacon or an acolyte leads the confession and the presider says the absolution.

The presider goes to the altar, if not already there, and says or sings the introduction to the Lord's Prayer. After the Lord's Prayer, the presider says "The gifts of God for the people of God" and administers communion. Lay ministers of communion may assist as at other times. When all have received, the remaining elements are consumed and the vessels removed to the sacristy or the credence table. The presider, standing at the altar or the chair, says or sings the final prayer, and all leave in silence. Servers may carry out the altar candles, leaving the altar dark and bare as it was at the beginning of the service.

4. Good Friday without a Priest

In the absence of a priest, a deacon or lay reader may conduct the Good Friday liturgy, except for the ministration of communion. A lay presider may wear alb or cassock and surplice. A deacon also wears a red stole. The service is conducted as described in section 6 above, ending with the veneration of the cross, the Lord's Prayer, and the final prayer.

The bishop may permit a deacon to distribute communion on this day. In that case it is done as in the previous section. A deacon or lay reader may also conduct the Way of the Cross or the daily offices.

Chapter Eight

Holy Saturday

Holy Saturday, also called the Holy Sabbath and the Great Sabbath, is an empty day, the day when Christ rested in the tomb and all creation awaited the resurrection. Only the daily offices are traditional, and Evening Prayer, unlike the custom on other festivals, is not the festal First Evensong of Easter, but a Holy Saturday office with a reading from Romans 8. *The Book of Common Prayer* has contained propers for a Liturgy of the Word on this day since 1549; neither the Roman nor Sarum Missal contained such a service. "There is no celebration of the Eucharist on this day" (BCP 283). The Word liturgy will normally be held in the morning or at noon, so that the church can be made ready for the Great Vigil.

The altar is bare, as on Good Friday, although in some places it is covered with the funeral pall. The wooden cross used on Good Friday remains in place. The presider wears an alb and Holy Week red stole. The presiding priest may wear a chasuble and the deacon a dalmatic. The entrance is in silence, without cross or candles. All bow to the altar and go to their places. The presider begins the liturgy with the salutation and the collect of the day, or the presider may say "Let us pray," and the deacon, "Let us kneel in silent prayer," followed by "Arise," after all have knelt and prayed briefly.

All sit while the reader goes to the lectern for the first reading. Psalm 31:1-5 may be read or sung. A reader reads the second lesson. After the second reading Psalm 130 may be read or sung as a tract. The deacon (or assisting priest, or the presider) takes the gospel book and goes to the place where the gospel is accustomed to be read, but without incense or lights. In *The Prayer Book Office*, Galley recommends announcing the gospel in the following way: "The conclusion of the Passion of our Lord Jesus Christ according to Matthew [or John]." If this is done, the usual responses are omitted.

After the gospel and homily, and in place of the Prayers of the People, the anthem from the Burial of the Dead "In the midst of life" (BCP 484/492) is sung or said (BCP 283). It may be sung or recited responsively. The presider then leads the congregation in the Lord's Prayer and the service concludes with the grace. All bow to the altar and leave in silence.

In the absence of a priest, a deacon or lay reader may preside.

EASTER
and the
GREAT
FIFTY DAYS

Chapter Nine

The Great Vigil of Easter

Easter, the Christian Passover, was originally a unitive feast, celebrating the passion and resurrection of Jesus Christ, and our participation therein. It included both a period of fasting and a rejoicing in Christ's victory and ours. This participation by the believer in the dying and rising again of Jesus Christ is the theological center of Christian faith and life. This is the gospel which the apostles proclaimed to the world, and it is our participation in the resurrection that makes us one with Jesus Christ. It is this proclamation which is central to the celebration of the Great Vigil of Easter. At the beginning of the Great Vigil the presider proclaims:

> Dear friends in Christ: On this most holy night, in which our Lord Jesus passed over from death to life, the Church invites her members, dispersed throughout the world, to gather in vigil and prayer. For this is the Passover of the Lord, in which, by hearing his Word and celebrating his Sacraments, we share in his victory over death. (BCP 285)

The Holy Week services carry us through the events of the passion. This more ancient service leads us from death to life with Christ through fire, light, word, water, and bread and wine. A new fire is kindled, a great candle is lighted, by its light the Bible is read, prayer and praise are offered, and we celebrate the Easter sacraments of baptism and eucharist. At the Great Vigil we celebrate the paschal mystery, which incorporates us into Christ's saving acts. John of Damascus, in his great Easter hymn, sings:

Come, ye faithful, raise the strain of triumphant gladness!
God hath brought his Israel into joy from sadness:
loosed from Pharaoh's bitter yoke Jacob's sons and daughters,
led them with unmoistened foot through the Red Sea waters.

'Tis the spring of souls today: Christ hath burst his prison,
and from three days' sleep in death as a sun hath risen;
all the winter of our sins, long and dark, is flying
from his light, to whom we give laud and praise undying.

(Hymn 199/200)

These two stanzas catch the spirit of the Great Vigil as a passage we are making in Word and Sacrament. Dom Odo Casel, the great Benedictine theologian of the Liturgical Movement, said of sacred mysteries, "The congregation, by performing the rite, take part in the saving act."[1] Clearly there is a sense in which we do just that at the Great Vigil. The mystery of Easter comes alive and we become a part of it.

The Vigil was already established in the fourth century. The pilgrim Egeria says of the Jerusalem Vigil only that it was just like the one back home. The tradition of holding a vigil of readings encompassing the whole history of salvation leading to a eucharist at the beginning of the Lord's Day, either at midnight or dawn, is very early. The incorporation of baptism

---

1. *The Mystery of Christian Worship*, ed. Bernard Neunheuser (Westminster, Md.: Newman Press, 1962), 52.

---

into the Vigil between the readings and the eucharist resulted from the fixing of Easter as the great baptismal feast, probably in the second or third century.

The decrease in adult candidates for baptism caused the beginning of the decline of the Great Vigil. In the Middle Ages it was moved to a more convenient hour: first to the afternoon, then to Saturday morning. In this form it survived until the Reformation, but it had ceased to be the focus of popular devotion. The Reformers simply abolished it, turning their attention to Easter morning, which had become the popular celebration of Easter. All that remained among Anglicans was the tradition of Easter Even baptisms.

The Easter Vigil, like the Holy Week services, was reintroduced in its Sarum form into Anglicanism in the nineteenth century in the wake of the Oxford Movement. In Massey Shepherd's *Holy Week Offices* a number of possible Easter Even schedules were included. These suggested the lighting of the paschal candle before Evening Prayer or a vigil, followed by baptism, and ante-communion in the afternoon. Shepherd also pointed out:

> In many places, however, there is a desire to return to the ancient "all-night" rite. In such cases, the liturgy should begin about 9:30 or 10:00 p.m., and conclude after midnight with the first Eucharist of Easter Day.[2]

It was in these forms that the Great Vigil began to make its way in the 1950s and 1960s from a small group of Anglo-Catholic parishes into the liturgical mainstream of the Episcopal Church. Except for the Blessing of the Paschal Candle, which appeared in the 1960 edition of *The Book of Offices*, the inclusion of the Easter Vigil in *Prayer Book Studies 19* in 1970 marked its official introduction into the liturgy of the Episcopal Church.

---

2. Shepherd, *Holy Week Offices* (Greenwich: Seabury Press, 1958), p. vii.

The restoration of the nighttime vigil in the Roman Catholic Church began in 1951, and a new rite containing the renewal of baptismal vows by the congregation was included in the 1956 revision of the Holy Week rites. The rite was further revised and translated into the vernacular after Vatican Council II.

In its present form, the Great Vigil consists of four parts:

(1) the Service of Light;
(2) the Service of Lessons;
(3) Christian Initiation; and
(4) the Holy Eucharist.

The Service of Light is a special form of the lamp lighting that was once a part of every evening service. In origin it is a utilitarian act: the service is at night, and light is needed. The service will be long, so a large light is needed. Yet it did not long remain a utilitarian act. Not only at the Vigil, but at every evening service, the bringing of light into the dark building was identified with the light of Christ shining in the darkness. At the Great Vigil the service begins with the lighting of a new fire. The ritual extinguishing of the old lights and the kindling of a new fire is an archetypal symbol of renewal and new birth. Before the invention of matches it was serious business to put out your source of light and kindle a new one. So the Great Vigil starts with this act of beginning anew, as reflected in the presider's prayer "that in this Paschal feast we may so burn with heavenly desires, that with pure minds we may attain to the festival of everlasting light" (BCP 285).

The deacon leads the congregation into the church, carrying the newly lighted candle and proclaiming it "The light of Christ." The candles of the congregation and the lights of the church are lighted from the new light. "The true light which enlightens everyone" is spread throughout the congregation (BCP 286). The *Exsultet* is a special example of the prayer for light which traditionally accompanies the lighting of the evening light. The deacon calls upon the angels, the whole earth, and "Mother Church" to rejoice in the resurrection of Christ and to sing the praise of "this marvelous and holy flame," which is its symbol, proclaiming, "This is the night...": the night of Passover, the night of resurrection, the night of our redemption, "when all who believe in Christ are delivered from the gloom of sin, and are restored to grace and holiness of life." The *Exsultet* celebrates not only the mighty acts of God in Moses and in Christ, but our own participation in these events through the Easter sacraments of baptism and eucharist.

By the light of this new fire the Hebrew Scriptures are read, beginning with the story of Creation, and including Israel's deliverance at the Red Sea. Each reading is followed by a psalm or canticle and a collect which gives a Christian context to the reading. As many as twelve lessons have been read at various times. The Prayer Book requires two and offers nine, permitting a shorter or a longer vigil. In origin these readings and their Christian interpretation in the collects following were a summary of the church's tradition as it was passed on to a new generation of Christians preparing for baptism. They sum up baptismal instruction and bring the central teachings of Christianity to the consciousness of those already baptized as we move to the celebration of the Easter sacraments.

After the readings the action moves to the font, where the water is blessed, the candidates are baptized, and the baptismal covenant is renewed by the congregation. Baptism is the theological climax of the Great Vigil.

> Do you not know that all of us who have been baptized into Christ Jesus were baptized into his death? Therefore we have been buried with him by baptism into death, so that, just as Christ was raised from the dead by the glory of the Father, so we too might walk in newness of life. For if we have been united with him in a death like his, we will certainly be united with him in a resurrection like his. (Rom. 6:3-5)

As we celebrate the resurrection of Christ and our own participation in that resurrection, we bring new members to share in that new life through the baptismal washing, that we and they may pass with Christ through death to life. The Vigil is also clearly an appropriate time for the reaffirmation of the Baptismal Covenant by the whole church, as we may remember that in the waters of baptism we made this passage with Christ.

Finally, the church, renewed and increased by the addition of the newly baptized, makes eucharist, as we join in celebrating the Easter eucharist and in receiving the Body and Blood of Christ. The bond of union with God in Christ established in the font is proclaimed in the reading from Romans 6. What has been hinted at in the readings from the Hebrew Scriptures is now made explicit in the resurrection gospel. The Body of Christ which is the church receives the Body of Christ which is the eucharist, and enters into the rejoicing of the Great Fifty Days united to its risen Head.

It is all there. Not with the drama of Palm Sunday and Good Friday, but with the solid symbols of faith, fire, light, water, bread and wine, and with the proclamation of the Word of God. In the Great Vigil of Easter we pass over with Christ from death to life, and with the church from Lent to Easter.

1. Preparing for the Great Vigil

A service as complex as the Great Vigil requires a substantial amount of planning. The first and most basic decision to be made is the place of the Great Vigil in the parish celebration of Easter. The Vigil can be celebrated quite effectively with a small group of people, but, if it is done this way in a large congregation, it will not be perceived as the principal liturgy of the year, which it clearly is theologically. If the Vigil is being introduced to a parish, it may be pastorally desirable to start small, but the service needs to reflect its importance. It needs to be self-evidently a major service, not an extra devotion for the pious. This means that an allocation of resources between the Great Vigil and the liturgy on Easter Day is necessary. If both cannot be done "all out" as great occasions, choices must be made which will reflect both the theology and the practicality of what is happening.

Many parishes have decided to place their highest priority on making the Vigil something special, with their best music and as much participation as possible. The Prayer Book says specifically that "it is customary for all the ordained ministers present, together with lay readers, singers, and other persons, to take active parts in the service" (BCP 284). The bishop, rector, vicar, or priest-in-charge is the appropriate presiding celebrant. Assisting priests may stand at the altar with the presider during the Great Thanksgiving, assist in the breaking of the bread, preach, and be eucharistic ministers, but they must not usurp the ministry of deacons or of lay persons. Only in the absence of deacons may they read the gospel and prepare the altar. It is usually not appropriate to have more than one priest recite the Great Thanksgiving, or parts thereof. If the parish has more than one deacon, their duties may be divided among them. The involvement of many lay people is also important. Different readers may be used for each lesson, for example, as well as different cantors and precentors. A reception for the newly baptized and the congregation may follow the service. Some parishes even use champagne as the altar wine for the service to increase the atmosphere of festivity.

The Vigil is celebrated "at a convenient time between sunset on Holy Saturday and sunrise on Easter Morning" (BCP 284). The most traditional times would be late in the evening, with the eucharist beginning at midnight, the beginning of "the first day of the week," or an hour or more before dawn, with the eucharist beginning at sunrise. In those places where Easter sunrise services are customary, the early morning option may be preferable. In the Jewish tradition the day began at sunset, and some congregations will choose to begin the vigil at sunset or soon after. It may conclude with the eucharist, or adjourn until dawn or a convenient early hour. In some Native American traditions, this is the usual way of keeping vigil. People take turns tending the fire, to keep it burning all night, and the rest sleep, rising for the ceremonies at daybreak. Some places will wish to schedule an "all-night" vigil, with homilies following all nine lessons and the gospel. Most places will choose an evening hour, and four to six lessons.

If at all possible, light the fire outdoors. It may be a large bonfire, or a small wood fire kindled in a brazier. In warmer climates, the fire can be lighted in a garden or cloister. If necessary it may be moved into the narthex, or even to the back of the nave, but extreme care must be taken to prevent the fire from spreading. A fire extinguisher should be conveniently at hand, in case of necessity. A small flashlight, placed near the fire or carried from the sacristy by the acolyte, may also prove helpful. Also needed near the fire are:

- A lighter or other device for lighting the fire;
- A taper for transferring the flame to the paschal candle;
- The empty thurible, if incense is to be used;
- The coals to be lighted in the fire and placed in the thurible;
- Tongs with which to move the burning coals;
- The paschal candle;
- A stylus, if symbols are to be inscribed on the candle;
- The five wax nails to be placed in the candle in the form of a cross;
- Candles to be given to the congregation, placed where the ushers can give them to people as they arrive.

The lectern from which the *Exsultet* will be sung and the lessons read may be placed in the center of the chancel or sanctuary. Near the lectern are placed:

- The stand for the paschal candle, so that it may give light to the book;
- The book containing the text (and music) of the *Exsultet* (on the lectern);
- The Bible or lectionary texts from which the lessons will be read nearby, so that it may be placed on the lectern after the *Exsultet*;
- Stands for processional torches, on either side of the lectern, to provide additional light.

The font is prepared for baptism. This requires:

- A ewer containing the water, unless the font is equipped with "living water," that is, running water;
- A baptismal shell, unless the baptisms will be by immersion;
- Sufficient towels, white garments, and baptismal candles for the newly baptized;
- A vat and sprinkler (which may be a branch) to sprinkle the congregation with the baptismal water;
- Chrism in an appropriate vessel or oil stock;
- A bowl with warm water and liquid detergent (or dry bread and a slice of lemon) for washing the presider's hands.

The altar is vested for Easter, with the best festal frontal. If the font is not at the front of the church, additional flowers and Easter decorations may be brought into the sanctuary during the baptisms, so that they will be seen when the procession returns to the altar for the eucharist. The lighting in the sanctuary is kept low until the beginning of the eucharist, when it is turned on so that the Easter joy is reflected in bright light.

The usual preparations for a Sunday eucharist are made. Festal white vestments are worn. The presider may wear alb and stole, or alb, stole, and cope, putting on the chasuble at the beginning of the eucharist.

2. The Lighting of the Paschal Candle

The church is dark, or as nearly so as practical, before the liturgy begins. The congregation assemble near the unlighted fire and are given unlighted candles. It is clearly preferable for the people to gather around the fire, even if the fire is in the back of the church, and to process behind the deacon into the church or to their places, than for them to be already in the pews. The ministers, the thurifer without the thurible, and the acolyte carrying a small flashlight gather near the fire. The presider lights the fire, using a lighter or flint, and addresses the congregation, using or adapting the form in the Prayer Book (BCP 285). If the fire does not give sufficient light for the presider, the acolyte may hold the flashlight. A deacon (or the acolyte, if not holding the flashlight) may hold the book. The presider, in the orans position, says or sings the prayer blessing the fire, making the sign of the cross at "Sanctify this new fire...." If incense is used, the coals are taken from the fire with tongs and placed in the thurible. The presider puts on incense and censes the fire.

The presider may prepare the paschal candle by cutting in the candle with a stylus a cross, the Greek letter *alpha* above the cross and *omega* below it, and the date in numerals between the arms of the cross. This is normally done by tracing a design already on the candle. This ceremony, introduced into the 1956 revision of the Roman Holy Week rites, is found also in the Canadian *Book of Alternative Services* (BAS 333) as an option. It is not in the American *Book of Common Prayer* and may be omitted. The candle may be decorated and the wax nails set in place before the service, or only the nails may be set in place at this time.

If the form in the Canadian book is followed, the presider says:

> 1. "Christ yesterday and today" (tracing the vertical arm of the cross);
> 2. "the beginning and the end" (tracing the horizonal arm);
> 3. "Alpha" (tracing α above the cross);
> 4. "and Omega" (tracing Ω below the cross);
> 5. "all time belongs to him" (tracing the first numeral of the year in the upper left corner of the cross);
> 6. "and all the ages" (tracing the second numeral in the upper right corner);
> 7. "to him be glory and power" (tracing the third numeral in the lower left corner);
> 8. "through every age for ever. Amen." (tracing the final numeral in the lower right corner).

Then the presider inserts the five wax nails into the candle in the form of a cross, saying, "By his holy and glorious wounds may Christ our Lord guard us and keep us. Amen."

The wax nails are called in the text "five grains of incense." The custom of inserting incense into the nails seems to have been derived from an overly literal reading of the *Exsultet,* which in early versions spoke of an evening sacrifice of incense. The nails are inserted beginning at the top and moving down the vertical arm, then the left and right horizontal nails are added. The presider then takes a taper and lights the paschal candle from the new fire, saying, "May the light of Christ, rising in glory, dispel the darkness of our hearts and minds" (BAS 333).

Alternatively, all preparations of the candle may be done in silence, and all but the lighting of the candle may be omitted.

The deacon then takes the lighted candle and leads the procession into the darkened church. If there are two deacons, one carries the candle, the other walks beside the presider. If the fire has been lighted at the back of the nave, the procession starts down the center aisle. All carry unlighted candles. If there is no deacon the presider or an assisting priest carries the paschal candle. The order of procession is:

(Thurifer)
Deacon carrying the paschal candle
Servers
Choir
Assisting clergy
Presider
Congregation.

At the back of the church (or at the back of the center aisle if the fire was lighted in the back of the church), a station is made. The deacon raises the candle and sings (or says), "The Light of Christ," to which all respond, "Thanks be to God." (The music for this is in *The Altar Book* and at S 68 in *The Hymnal 1982.*) The servers light their candles from the paschal candle and light the candles of the presider and the assisting clergy. As the procession moves down the aisle the light is passed from candle to candle until the candles of all in the procession are lighted. A second station is made in the middle of the church, and the deacon repeats the acclamation at a higher pitch. A third station is made at the head of the aisle and the acclamation repeated at a still higher pitch.

The deacon then places the paschal candle in its stand near the lectern. Torches on either side of the lectern may be lighted, and all other candles, except those near or on the altar, are lighted. The congregation go to their places as the procession moves down the aisle, and those in the sanctuary go to their places after the third station. The thurifer brings incense to the presider, who puts incense in the thurible and blesses it. The thurifer gives the thurible to the deacon, who censes the paschal candle. The deacon returns the thurible to the thurifer, goes to the lectern, and sings the *Exsultet*. (Music for the *Exsultet* is in *The Altar Book.*) All stand, holding their candles. The acolyte stands beside the deacon to turn pages, hold a flashlight or hand candle, or do whatever is necessary. If the people do not need the light of the candles to see, they may extinguish them at the end of the *Exsultet*, and relight them for the baptism.

If a deacon is unable to sing the *Exsultet*, some other person, such as a member of the choir, may do so. In this case the deacon stands beside the actual singer at the lectern and turns the pages. Others contend that if a deacon is present, no matter how badly he or she sings, the deacon should sing the *Exsultet*.

3. The Liturgy of the Word

At the conclusion of the *Exsultet* the deacon goes to the right of the presider. The presider, facing the people, introduces the Scripture lessons. The substitution of "similar words" for the introduction printed in *The Book of Common Prayer* is permitted (BCP 288). All sit for the readings. The first reader goes to the lectern and reads the first lesson. The church may remain darkened, but there must be sufficient light at the lectern for the reader to see. A different reader reads each lesson, with the usual announcement and conclusion. Some congregations will wish to vary the manner in which the lessons are read. The readings may, for example, be told as stories. Some may be acted out, perhaps by children in costume. Different voices may be used in some readings, such as the voice of God in the creation story. In some settings, pictures may be projected on the wall during the reading. Other creative variations are possible.[3]

At the conclusion of each reading there is a psalm or canticle. These may be said or sung in any of the ways used for the psalm at the eucharist. They need not all be sung in the same way. Some may be sung by the choir to more difficult or anthem settings. One or more may be sung by the congregation to metrical settings.

"The priests who are present share among them the reading of the Collects which follow each Lesson" (BCP 284). If no other priests are present, the presider says all of the collects. If there are assisting priests the collects are distributed among them. If there are fewer priests than collects, the presider reads the collect after the last lesson.

At the end of the psalm or canticle all stand. The priest says, "Let us pray," pauses to give the people an opportunity to do so, then says (or sings) the collect. This pattern is repeated after each reading. If a homily is preached after any of the readings, it follows the reading immediately, and the psalm or canticle follows the homily.

---

3. See Joseph P. Russell, *The New Prayer Book Guide to Christian Education* (Cambridge, Mass.: Cowley Publications, 1996), pp. 98-101.

---

4. The Celebration of Holy Baptism

The traditional place for the celebration of Holy Baptism is immediately following the Vigil readings. It may, however, be celebrated after the gospel and sermon of the eucharist, as on other occasions. If that is to be done, the altar candles are now lighted, the lights of the sanctuary turned on, and the Easter eucharist begun. It is more dramatic and follows the unfolding of the Vigil rite better to move from the lectern to the font to the altar. We are instructed in the Word of God, we respond by coming to the font where we become partakers of Christ's dying and rising again, then we listen to the Easter gospel proclaiming the resurrection and come to the Lord's table to make eucharist. Baptism celebrates our passing over with Christ from death to life, and it is the point of the Vigil liturgy when we sacramentally celebrate the resurrection, and then we move to the proclamation of the Easter joy. Dramatically, this order turns the focus away from the sanctuary to the font to pass through the waters of death with Christ, so that the procession from the font can go to the altar singing the Easter canticles and entering the joy of the resurrection. Placing the baptism after the gospel and sermon sees the baptism as a response to the Easter gospel, keeps all of the readings together, and is closer to the usual Sunday format. In this order the baptism leads directly to the peace and the offertory so that it becomes the sacramental embodiment of the Easter gospel just proclaimed and moves directly from font to altar.

a. The Presentation of Candidates

Holy Baptism begins with the presentation of the candidates on page 301 of *The Book of Common Prayer*. This usually takes place at the chancel steps, unless it is possible for the entire congregation to move to the font and see and hear what is being done there. In that case the presentation and examination may take place at the font, and the procession to the font as described below takes places now. Psalm 42:1-7 is fittingly sung during the procession.

The presider comes to the center of the chancel steps. The deacon stands to the celebrant's right, and the acolyte or another deacon with the book to the left. The candidates and sponsors come forward and stand facing the presider. It is helpful if they stand to the left and right so that the people can see the presider.

Adults and older children are presented first. After each presentation the candidate is asked, "Do you desire to be baptized?" Infants are then presented. The presider questions all the parents and godparents together after all have been presented. The presider then asks all the candidates to make the renunciations of evil and the acceptance of Jesus Christ. All candidates able to answer for themselves and the sponsors of infant candidates respond together (BCP 302). If there are candidates for confirmation, reception, or reaffirmation, they are then presented. This will normally only happen if the bishop is the presider.

b. The Renewal of Baptismal Vows

The presider asks the congregation to support the candidates in their life in Christ and invites them to join the candidates who are entering the baptismal covenant and renew their own baptismal vows. The invitation to the people to renew their vows in the Easter Vigil (BCP 292) may precede the invitation in the baptismal rite (BCP 303), or since the rubrics permit the use of "similar words" for both, they may easily be combined by adding the phrase "to join with *those* who *are* committing *themselves* to Christ and..." to the invitation in the Vigil:

> I call upon you, therefore, now that our Lenten observance is ended, to join with *those* who *are* committing *themselves* to Christ and to renew the solemn promises and vows of Holy Baptism.... (BCP 292)

c. The Procession to the Font

If they are not already at the font, the procession to the font forms in this order:

Deacon with the paschal candle

(Choir)

Servers

(Assisting Clergy)

Acolyte

Presider

Candidates and Sponsors

(Congregation).

If it is possible, it is desirable to have the congregation join in the procession and gather around the font. Everyone relights their candles and holds them during the procession and the baptisms: ushers or servers take the light from the paschal candle and distribute it as expeditiously as possible. If the space is limited, the congregation may remain in the pews and face the font, and the choir may remain in their places. During the procession the person appointed sings the Prayers for the Candidates (BCP 305). This may be a member of the choir, or a sponsor, or anyone else capable of doing so. When the procession arrives at the font the presider sings the final collect (BCP 306). If the font is in a baptistry, the presider sings the collect at the entrance to the baptistry.

Alternatively, Psalm 42:1-7 or a hymn may be sung during the procession. Hymn 658 is a metrical version of the psalm. In this case the Prayers for the Candidates are said or sung after all have arrived at the font and are in place, concluding with the presider's collect.

d. The Baptism

The presider stands facing the congregation across the font. The deacon holding the paschal candle stands a few steps to the right. The acolyte (or another deacon) stands to the celebrant's left. Unless the book is placed on a stand, the acolyte or a deacon may hold it.

The presider (or an assisting minister) pours water into the font, unless the font has "living," that is, running, water. It the font is large enough that it must be filled before the baptism, the presider may still pour water from a single symbolic ewer into the font before the thanksgiving. The presider sings, or says, the Thanksgiving over the Water (BCP 306). At the words "Now sanctify this water..." the presider touches the water, making the sign of the cross. Alternatively, the presider may take the paschal candle from the deacon and lower its base into the font, repeating the action three times and singing or saying the phrase "Now sanctify this water, we pray you, by the power of your Holy Spirit" three times in successively higher pitches, as explained in *The Altar Book*. The acolyte dries the bottom of the candle with a towel. The presider returns it to the deacon and continues the prayer. The presider may cense the font following the Thanksgiving over the Water.

Unless the bishop is the presider and will consecrate chrism at this time, the baptisms immediately follow the Thanksgiving over the Water. The presider may baptize the candidates, or an assisting priest or deacon may do so. If the number of candidates is large, more than one minister may baptize. Each candidate is immersed, or water is poured over his or her head three times while the baptizing minister says:

N., I baptize you in the Name of the Father, and of the Son, and of the Holy Spirit. Amen. (BCP 307)

If the baptisms have been by immersion or total affusion, a psalm or hymn may be sung while the candidates are clothed in their baptismal robes. If the candidates are not infants, they retire to an appropriate facility to take off wet clothing and put on the white baptismal robes.

The acolyte may light a candle from the paschal candle following each baptism and give it to the presider, who gives it to the newly baptized or to a godparent.

e. The Consignation and Chrismation

A server may fill the vat with water from the baptismal font and put the sprinkler (which may be a sprig of evergreen) into it and hand it to the priest. The priest sprinkles the congregation with the baptismal water. If the presider can be clearly seen by the congregation while remaining near the font, the consignation may take place there, and the returning procession be delayed until after that action. Otherwise the procession now returns to the chancel step in the order in which it went to the font. The newly baptized carry their candles, or their godparents carry them for them. The procession may take place in silence, or Psalm 23, or a metrical version thereof, may be sung. The deacon returns the paschal candle to its stand and stands at the presider's right. All take their places as for the presentation and Baptismal Covenant.

The presider, "at a place in full sight of the congregation" (BCP 308), extends both hands with palms down toward the candidates and says the prayer of the consignation (BCP 308). The acolyte holds the book. The presider goes to each candidate in turn, or they come to the presider if it is more convenient.

Normally the laying on of hands and anointing are done in one of the following ways:

1. The priest takes the vessel of chrism, pours a small amount of it into the palm of the right hand, places the hand against the person's forehead, and spreads the chrism across the forehead (and, if desired, down the person's cheeks) while reciting the words, "N., you are sealed by the Holy Spirit in Baptism." Then, while saying the words, "and marked as Christ's own for ever," the priest traces a cross on the person's forehead with the thumb.

2. The priest dips the right thumb into the chrism or touches the oil stock with it. Then, laying the hand on the person's head, traces a cross on the forehead with the thumb while saying the prescribed formula.[4]

Another possibility, making more extensive use of chrism, is to pour the chrism from a glass vessel over the head of the newly baptized, spread it with the hand, and make the sign of the cross on the forehead in the oil. This is almost certainly the method used in the early church.

The consignation and chrismation are significant acts of the baptismal liturgy and deserve to be performed in a manner that makes this clear. The signing with the cross (consignation) is a vivid sign of our membership in Christ. The mark of the Good Shepherd is placed on the foreheads of the sheep, marking us "as Christ's own for ever." It is "the seal of the living God" which marks the foreheads of God's servants (Rev. 7:1-3). The chrism is not only the "paint" with which the sign is applied, it is itself a powerful symbol of union with Christ. The prayer for the consecration of the chrism prays "that those who are sealed with it may share in the royal priesthood of Jesus Christ" (BCP 307). As Christ was anointed by the Holy Spirit at his baptism, so are Christians anointed in union with the Anointed One at theirs, signifying that we are members of the royal priesthood which is the holy people of God (1 Peter 2:9).

If the chrism is not used, the presider lays the hand on the person's head, and traces the cross on the forehead while saying the formula.

After all have been anointed a server brings the bowl of warm water to the presider, who washes his or her hand to remove the oil.

All join in welcoming the newly baptized. If the procession has not yet returned to the chancel it does so now. The priest may say the Easter acclamation from the font and the procession return to the sanctuary singing the opening canticle of the Easter eucharist.

---

4. Galley, *The Ceremonies of the Eucharist*, 180.

---

5. The Renewal of Baptismal Vows

If there is no baptism the congregation still renew their baptismal vows as provided in *The Book of Common Prayer* on pages 292-294. It is appropriate to process to the font after the psalm and collect at the end of the final reading, and to bless the baptismal water.

The procession goes to the font while Psalm 42:1-7 is sung. The presider says the Thanksgiving over the Water as in the previous section. The presider invites the congregation to renew their baptismal vows and leads them in doing so. A server gives the vat filled with baptismal water to the presider, who sprinkles the people with the water. The procession returns to the sanctuary, either in silence or singing Psalm 23 or an appropriate hymn. Alternatively, the presider may say the Easter acclamation and the procession return to the sanctuary singing the opening canticle of the Easter eucharist.

6. The First Eucharist of Easter

Following the welcoming of the newly baptized, the presider may say (or sing) the Easter acclamation, "Alleluia. Christ is risen." Bells are rung, the organ sounds, and *Gloria in excelsis*, *Te Deum laudamus*, or *Pascha nostrum* is sung. In many congregations the people bring bells with them to ring at this time. The acclamation may be omitted and the festivity begin with the canticle. This should mark a distinctive change in the service. The altar candles are lighted from the paschal candle, the lighting in the sanctuary is turned on, and the sound of joy fills the church. Any remaining Lenten veils are removed. Baptism celebrates our passage with Christ from death to life and our passage with the church from the paschal fast to the paschal feast.

If the baptisms or renewal of vows are completed at the font, the procession may return to the sanctuary singing the canticle. If the procession has already returned to the chancel step for the consignation, the acclamation is said from there and the canticle begun. If the baptisms are to be celebrated after the gospel, the presider sings the acclamation from the chair and all proceeds as described.

If the presider is not wearing a chasuble, it is put on before the end of the canticle. The presider, facing the congregation from the chair, sings, "The Lord be with you," and the collect. The second collect, "O God, who made this most holy night to shine with the glory of the Lord's resurrection...," is usually preferable, and especially so if baptism is administered. There is no Old Testament reading, since the Hebrew Scriptures have been read during the Service of Lessons. A lector reads the epistle from Romans 6.

The Easter Alleluia is traditionally sung after the epistle. (The music is in *The Altar Book* and at S 70 in *The Hymnal 1982*.) "Alleluia" is sung by the presider or someone else, such as a cantor, and repeated by the choir and congregation. This is done three times at successively higher pitches. This may be followed by Psalm 114 or a hymn.

The gospel procession is formed in the usual way, and the deacon sings or reads the resurrection account from the Gospel according to St. Matthew. The major sermon of the Great Vigil follows the gospel. The Nicene Creed is omitted (BCP 295), since the Apostles' Creed is part of the Baptismal Covenant.

If baptism or the renewal of baptismal vows was not celebrated earlier, it may take place here. All is done as described above, except that Psalm 23 or a hymn accompany the procession back from the font.

The celebration continues with the Prayers of the People (BCP 295). A deacon or other person appointed leads the prayers, and the presider says or sings the final collect.

The eucharist continues in the customary Sunday manner, with the exchange of the Peace. Eucharistic Prayer A (with the Easter preface) or Prayer D (which has its own preface) are most appropriate. Other priests participating in the liturgy may stand at the altar with the presider, as provided in *The Book of Common Prayer*. It is not appropriate for them to recite sections of the eucharistic prayer, or to usurp the function of the deacon(s).

After the postcommunion prayer the presider, standing at the chair or at the altar, says or sings the fourfold Easter seasonal blessing from *The Book of Occasional Services* (BOS 26) with arms extended toward the people, palms down. (This gesture is optional and may be omitted.) The sign of the cross is made at the final Trinitarian blessing.

The deacon adds "Alleluia, Alleluia" after the words of the dismissal, and the congregation responds, "Thanks be to God. Alleluia, Alleluia."

The Prayer Book expects the dismissal to follow the blessing at once and the service to end without a processional hymn. In fact, in many places the procession forms after the blessing, and the deacon either remains in the sanctuary to give the dismissal after the hymn, or gives the dismissal from the back of the church after the hymn. However "unrubrical" these practices may be, they preserve the point that the people leave when they are dismissed, rather than waiting for a hymn, the extinguishing of the candles, or additional prayers.

7. The Great Vigil in Small Congregations

Often those whose only experience of the Great Vigil has been in a large church with many clergy and excellent musical resources are unwilling even to try to celebrate the Vigil with a small congregation, but the Easter Vigil can be celebrated effectively by a small group of people. The minimum requirements are a priest, a reader, a cantor, an acolyte, one additional server, and a group of worshipers. A deacon and one or more candidates for baptism are desirable, and additional readers and musicians are helpful. In a very small congregation, everyone can have a liturgical role. The service may be celebrated quite informally, or it may be as formal as a large service.

a. Preparations

Special preparations for the Great Vigil need to be made at the place where the fire will be lighted, at the lectern, and at the baptismal font.

If the fire is to be lit outdoors, a fire of sticks may be kindled in a grill—or, if space and safety permit, a larger fire may be built in a fire ring. Indoors the fire may be set in an hibachi, or similar container. If the fire is lighted inside, it should be taken outdoors as soon as the paschal candle is lighted. Someone should be given a fire extinguisher and made responsible for seeing that the fire poses no danger. On a table near the fire are placed:

- The paschal candle;
- A lighter, or other device for lighting the fire;
- A taper for transferring the flame to the candle;
- Candles to be given to everyone present.

At the lectern are placed:

- A book containing the text (and music) for the *Exsultet;*
- A Bible or lectionary texts for reading the lessons;
- Stands for torches, or some other light source;
- The stand for the paschal candle.

Near the baptismal font are placed:

- A ewer of water;
- The book (or a Prayer Book) containing the Thanksgiving over the Water;
- A vat and sprinkler (which may be an evergreen branch) for sprinkling the people with the baptismal water.

If there is a baptism these items are also placed near the font:

- Towels for the newly baptized;
- White baptismal robes (if they are used) and baptismal candles for the newly baptized;
- A baptismal shell;
- The chrism and a bowl of warm water for the presider's hands.

The altar is vested for a major feast. Flowers and other ornaments may be in place, or they may be brought in at the beginning of the eucharist. Everything is prepared for a Sunday eucharist. The altar candles are not lighted.

b. The Lighting of the Paschal Candle

The church is as dark as is practical. The congregation gather near the fire. Candles are distributed to them. At the appropriate time, the priest, deacon, servers, and musicians gather near the fire. The acolyte brings a flashlight and the priest *The Book of Common Prayer.* The priest lights the fire with a lighter or flint, and reads the introductory address to the people. The priest says the prayer of blessing over the fire, making the sign of the cross at "Sanctify this new fire...."

If the priest is to mark the candle, it is done as described above, following the rite of the Canadian *Book of Alternative Services.* The candle may also be prepared before the service. The priest lights the candle with the taper, and, carrying the candle, leads the congregation into the church. If there is a deacon, the deacon takes the candle, and the presider walks at the end of the procession. The procession halts three times, as described above, the candle is raised, and "The light of Christ" sung. After the first station, the candles of the people are lit as the procession moves to the front of the church. After the final station, other candles in the church, except those on or near the altar, are lit, and the electric lights may be turned on enough to enable people to see to read. If possible, electric lights are kept low until the beginning of the eucharist.

The candle is placed in its stand near the lectern. The deacon or presider censes the candle, if incense is used. The *Exsultet* is sung rather than read, if at all possible. If no deacon is present, it may be sung by any person able to do so. If the singer is not already vested for a liturgical role in the service, an alb is an appropriate vesture. The presider, if not singing the *Exsultet*, goes to the chair. If the congregation is very small, they may stand around the candle. If it is larger, they stand at their places in the nave. After the *Exsultet* the people may extinguish their candles, if they are not needed for light.

c. The Liturgy of the Word

The presider introduces the Scripture readings, facing the congregation from the chair. The first reader goes to the lectern and reads the first lesson, announcing it in the usual way and saying, "The Word of the Lord," at the end. A single cantor may sing the verses of the psalm and the congregation respond with the refrain, as in *Gradual Psalms*, or the psalm may be sung in unison to simplified Anglican chants, or the psalm may be recited or sung in whatever way is customary at the Sunday eucharist. The presider says the collect after the psalm, pausing for silent prayer after "Let us pray." The remaining lessons are read in the same way. At least two lessons, including the reading from Exodus, are required. Usually four to six lessons are used. The length of the Vigil is largely determined by the number of lessons read.

d. The Baptism

If there are candidates for baptism, they are now presented. This may be done either at the font or at the chancel step. If the entire baptismal service is to be held at the font, the procession moves to the font following the collect after the last reading. A deacon or server leads the procession carrying the paschal candle; the other servers, choir members, the acolyte and the presider follow, with the candidates, sponsors, and (if possible) the congregation. This need not be a formal procession: the paschal candle may lead the deacon, presider, and acolyte to the font and everyone else come from their places to join them at the celebrant's invitation. A psalm or hymn may be sung to cover the movement to the font whether or not it is a formal procession. Psalm 42 or Hymn 658 (a metrical version of the psalm) are especially appropriate. If the first part of the baptismal rite is held at the front of the church, at the chancel step or similar location, the candidates, sponsors, and parents come forward and stand facing the presider. They should stand in such as way that the congregation can see the presider.

The presentation and examination take place as above, followed by the Baptismal Covenant, which all who are present renew with those taking it for the first time. The paschal invitation to do this may be used, altering it as indicated above in section 9.4b.

If the procession to the font has not yet taken place, it occurs during or before the Prayers for the Candidates (BCP 305). The Prayers for the Candidates may be led by a sponsor. If they are not sung during the movement to the font, they are said when all are in place. The presider says the final prayer, fills the font with water, and says or sings the Thanksgiving over the Water, facing the people across the font. If the baptisms are to be by immersion, see the description in section 9.4d above.

The presider (or an assisting priest or deacon) baptizes the candidates in the usual way. It is especially appropriate at the Great Vigil to give baptismal candles lighted from the paschal candle to the newly baptized. After the last baptism, the acolyte may fill the vat with baptismal water and the presider sprinkle the congregation with the water, using an evergreen green branch or a sprinkler.

If the consignation may be performed "in full sight of the congregation" at the font, then the presider proceeds to the prayer over the candidates. If it is necessary, the procession may move back to the chancel step before doing this, singing Psalm 23, or one of the many metrical versions of it, during the procession. The presider extends the arms, with palms down, over the candidates and says the prayer. The acolyte holds the book. The priest takes the chrism (if it is to be used) and anoints the candidates as described above. If chrism is not used, the priest places a hand on the head of each candidate and says the consignation formula, making the sign of the cross on the forehead of each. When this has been done for all candidates, the presider invites the congregation to welcome the newly baptized. All recite the welcome together (BCP 308).

If there are no baptisms, the presider may still go to the font (after the final lesson with its psalm and collect) and bless the water, then lead the congregation in the Renewal of Baptismal Vows (BCP 292) from a place near the font, concluding with the Easter acclamation.

e. The Easter Eucharist

After the welcome of the newly baptized or the renewal of baptismal vows, the presider says or sings the Easter acclamation, "Alleluia. Christ is risen," and the eucharist begins with the singing of a canticle. Bells and organ music are appropriate at this time to celebrate the Easter joy. If the baptismal procession has not returned to the sanctuary, they do so during the canticle. At the Easter acclamation, the lights in the sanctuary are turned on and the altar candles lit. If the presider is not wearing a chasuble, it is put on now.

After the canticle the presider goes to the chair, or to whatever place is customary, and says the collect; the second collect is especially suitable for the Vigil. The service continues in the manner of the Sunday eucharist with the following special features:

- "Alleluia" may be sung and repeated a total of three times before the gospel. If it is not sung, it may be said by the deacon or presider and repeated by the congregation. Each time the pitch and volume are higher.
- The Nicene Creed is omitted, since the Apostles' Creed was a part of the Baptismal Covenant.
- If baptism, or the renewal of vows, did not take place earlier, it may follow the gospel and sermon.
- The Easter seasonal blessing from *The Book of Occasional Services* may be used.
- Two Alleluias are added after the words of the dismissal and its response.

8. The Great Vigil without a Priest

It is clearly impossible to celebrate the Great Vigil without a priest to preside at the Easter eucharist, and congregations without a priest should make every effort to find one for this service. If the Great Vigil is omitted, the paschal candle may be blessed by the priest before the first eucharist on Easter Day.

The Book of Common Prayer does permit a deacon or lay reader to lead the first two parts of the service, the Renewal of Baptismal Vows, and the Ministry of the Word. A deacon wears an alb, stole, and white dalmatic (if one is available). A lay reader wears an alb, or a cassock and surplice. They follow the form described above, using as many lay assistants, readers, singers, and so forth as are available. The bishop may specially authorize a deacon to preside at baptism on this occasion (BCP 312). Note that specific permission of the bishop must be obtained. If that is done, the deacon omits the consignation and chrismation, and the prayers associated with it, moving directly to the welcoming of the newly baptized. There is almost no way to keep the celebration of the Vigil Ministry of the Word from seeming anti-climactic, and if it has to be done, it may be better to place the baptism or renewal of vows after the gospel and homily, so that they become the climax of the service. The service concludes with the Prayers of the People, the Lord's Prayer, and the dismissal (BCP 284).

It would certainly be better to hold the service at a different hour when a priest could be present, or to join with a neighboring congregation in celebrating the Vigil with a priest.

Chapter Ten

The Great Fifty Days

Pentecost originally meant the entire fifty-day period from the *Pascha* to the Feast of Pentecost. It was celebrated as one great season of rejoicing, an extended Lord's Day, on which there was no fasting and no kneeling. Easter, of course, has its origin in the Jewish Passover, at which Jesus died and rose again, so that all of the content of the Old Testament *Pascha* is carried over into the New, and the Christian meanings focused on the dying and rising again of Jesus are added to the old meanings. Christians saw the Old Testament Passover in the light of the Christian Passover, the death and resurrection of Christ, and our participation therein. We saw this expressed in the Great Vigil in the use of the Old Testament readings and the Christian collects.

In our calendar Easter Day is the Sunday after the first full moon of spring. It therefore falls between March 22 and April 25. The Great Fifty Days correspond to the Hebrew Feast of Weeks, which counted a week of weeks (forty-nine days) from Passover and celebrated the fiftieth day as

Shavuot or Pentecost. The Jewish Pentecost was an agricultural festival in origin, but it came to be celebrated as the feast of the giving of the Law to Moses on Sinai. Originally Christians considered all fifty days equal: each celebrated the resurrection and ascension of Christ and the descent of the Holy Spirit. The Great Fifty Days were, after the Paschal Vigil, the most appropriate time for baptism.

As Easter was considered by patristic authors to be both the first and the eighth day, the beginning of the week and its eschatological end, so the Pentecost began and ended with Sundays. In contemporary terminology Whitsunday is the Eighth Sunday of Easter, and it moves us into the eschatological dimension. As St. Basil wrote, "All of Pentecost reminds us of the resurrection which we await in the other world."

By the fourth century, the historicization that occurred in connection with Holy Week had its effect on the Great Fifty Days as well. Easter was the day of resurrection, Pentecost the day of the ascension and the descent of the Spirit. Egeria describes how on the morning of the Fiftieth Day in Jerusalem the congregation assembled at the third hour in the basilica called Sion, the place and time of the descent of the Holy Spirit, and in the afternoon went to the Imbomon on the Mount of Olives, the place of the ascension. By the last quarter of the century, Ascension Day was observed on a Thursday, the fortieth day after Easter, following the chronology of Acts. Chrysostom and Augustine both regarded it as universally observed.

The Great Fifty Days are the season of mystagogy. The great catechetical preachers of the fourth century, including Ambrose and Cyril, preached their sermons on the meaning of the sacraments and the new life in Christ (mystagogy) to the newly baptized on the weekdays of Easter Week.[1] The neophytes gathered in the church for the eucharist in their baptismal robes, accompanied by many of the faithful, to hear these sermons and to celebrate the eucharist. Egeria tells us that in Jerusalem the bishop deliv-

---

1. Passages from a number of these sermons may be found in Wright, *Readings for the Daily Office.*

---

ered these addresses seated in the door of the *anastasis*, the shrine built over the empty tomb.

1. The Easter Season

The Easter Season, the contemporary equivalent of the ancient Pentecost, begins with the Great Vigil and extends through the last service on the Day of Pentecost. The paschal candle is lighted at all services throughout the Great Fifty Days (BCP 287). The custom of extinguishing the candle at the gospel on Ascension Day has been abandoned, since it obscured the unity of the Great Fifty Days and suggested that Ascension Day began a new season.

The proper Easter acclamation is used at the eucharist and may begin the offices. "Alleluia, alleluia" is added to the dismissal both at the eucharist and the offices. Fraction anthems including Alleluias are chosen. Hymns with multiple Alleluias are sung. The Easter preface is used until Ascension Day, and then the Ascension preface is used until the Day of Pentecost, which has its own preface. It is therefore useful to use eucharistic prayers which permit the insertion of a proper preface at this time. (Eucharistic Prayers C and D do not.) The reference to the supper at Emmaus in Eucharistic Prayer C makes it especially suitable for use on the evening of Easter Day, Wednesday in Easter Week, and the Third Sunday of Easter in Year A.

The Easter seasonal blessing from *The Book of Occasional Services* (BOS 26-27) may be used throughout the season. In many congregations the Confession of Sin is omitted entirely during the whole Fifty Days, or replaced by a petition for absolution in the Prayers of the People (as in Form 1 or Form 5). In some places the Council of Nicea's prohibition on kneeling is followed and everyone stands for those parts of the liturgy during which they are accustomed to kneel at other times, including the Great Thanksgiving and the reception of communion. *The Book of Com-*

mon Prayer follows Nicea in exempting the Great Fifty Days from fasting (BCP 17).

The Great Fifty Days remains a baptismal season. The entire fifty days are used for mystagogy, and adults baptized at the Great Vigil may continue to sit together at the liturgy and to be prayed for by name (BOS 116). Even when there are no adult neophytes, the Easter season is a good time to teach the meaning of the sacraments and of living the new life of the resurrection. This is encouraged by the propers for the season.

A lesson from the Acts of the Apostles is appointed for every day during the Great Fifty Days and should always be used. The Old Testament readings assigned as alternatives on the Sundays of Easter are intended for use when Morning Prayer is used for the Liturgy of the Word. If the Old Testament reading is used at the Sunday eucharist, the lesson from Acts replaces the epistle. The propers for the weekdays of Easter Week are in *The Book of Common Prayer,* and major festivals must be transferred to the following week. Propers for the remainder of the season are in *Lesser Feasts and Fasts.* The readings are from Acts and the Gospel of John. Unlike Lent, priority is given after Easter Week to celebrating the festivals of the saints, and their propers regularly displace the weekday propers, "since the triumphs of the saints are a continuation and manifestation of the Paschal victory of Christ" (LFF 64). As in Lent, if there is not a daily celebration, the weekday propers may be chosen from any selection for the week.

The Easter invitatory *Pascha nostrum* is said every day during Easter Week in place of the *Venite* at Morning Prayer, and may be so used daily through Pentecost. It may also be used as an alternative to the *Gloria in excelsis* at the eucharist, which is used on all the Sundays and daily throughout Easter Week, and may be used daily for the whole fifty days (BCP 406). Another alternative to the *Gloria* is the canticle "This is the feast of victory for our God" (Hymnal 417/418). It is used in this way in the *Lutheran Book of Worship.*

The church is adorned for the Great Vigil and Easter Day with spring flowers and other appropriate symbols of the resurrection, and this practice continues throughout the season. The altar hangings and vestments are the best festal set. This is usually white, but may be gold or silver, or (for the hangings and stoles) a tapestry. Upholstery material is not really suitable for garments such as chasubles and dalmatics and is better used as orphreys. After the Great Vigil the stand for the paschal candle is placed on the liturgical north side of the sanctuary, near the altar, but not blocking sight lines or the movement of the ministers.

2. Easter Day

The services of Easter Day should be festive celebrations, even in congregations where the Great Vigil is the primary Easter celebration. It is important that, in an effort to emphasize the Great Vigil, the Easter Day services are not so scaled down as to make those who attend them feel slighted. Although some would suggest that nothing else is needed after the Great Vigil (except sleep), there are few congregations which do not feel the need to have services on Easter Day.

For some people Easter morning is the occasion of an infrequent visit to the church, and the eucharist of Easter Day is an opportunity to hear the gospel anew. For many regular churchgoers the Great Vigil has had no place in their devotional background and the service on Easter morning is for them the primary celebration of the major Christian festival. Others will wish to return after the Vigil for another, and to their mind more traditional, Easter service. Some will simply be unable to attend the Vigil and wish to worship on Easter Day. All need to feel that something important is happening, as indeed it is. The church is celebrating the resurrection of Jesus Christ.

The paschal celebration does begin at the Great Vigil, but it continues for fifty days, of which Easter Day is the first. In fact, the church celebrates the resurrection of Christ every Lord's Day, and the Easter liturgies should encourage all those who attend to participate weekly. The singing of familiar Easter hymns and the use of incense, banners, processional torches, or whatever the congregation associates with major festivals should be included. In many places, it is desirable to have additional baptisms at the principal Easter Day service, particularly the baptisms of infants, if adults are baptized at the Vigil. If there are no baptisms, the Renewal of Baptismal Vows from the Vigil replaces the Nicene Creed at the eucharist, and is introduced by the address on page 292 of the Prayer Book. After the concluding collect, the presider may sprinkle the people with the baptismal water blessed at the Great Vigil. The names of all those baptized at Easter are included in the Prayers of the People, or in the intercessions of Eucharistic Prayer D.

A separate set of propers for an evening service is included in *The Book of Common Prayer.* Howard Galley included in *The Prayer Book Office* a form for Great Paschal Vespers, a variation on Solemn Evensong for Easter Day and Easter Week. It includes the *lucernarium*, the sprinkling of the congregation with baptismal water, and a procession to the rood. It is a "cathedral" or parochial, rather than monastic, form of the office, and is a reasonable evening service for Easter Day for parishes with sufficient resources to mount a solemn evening office on Easter. His book contains detailed ceremonial directions, but no music. The psalms may, of course, be sung in the usual way.

3. Ascension Day

Ascension Day is celebrated on the fortieth day after Easter, following the chronology of Acts. It is a major feast, with an excellent selection of hymns provided in *The Hymnal 1982*. Since Ascension Day will almost inevitably be a working day, the principal celebration will probably be in the evening. Every effort should be made to have a service with music and to sing the popular and singable Ascension Day hymns. Boone Porter suggested some years ago in *Keeping the Church Year* that it was an excellent opportunity for a parish supper, and in many climates, it is an opportunity to have an outdoor service on a spring evening.

There are no particular ceremonies associated with the day; it is a part of the Great Fifty Days. It shows forth the glory of the risen Christ as he takes his place "at the right hand of the Father." This is symbolic language, and the emphasis is on the glorification of Christ in his risen humanity rather than on celestial architecture. The line from the preface, "that where he is, there we might also be, and reign with him in glory," expresses the heart of what we are celebrating. The paschal candle continues to burn until Pentecost. The weekday propers in *Lesser Feasts and Fasts* continue. The Ascension preface replaces that of Easter until Pentecost.

The religious term "Novena" derives from the description in Acts of the apostles passing the nine days between the Ascension and Pentecost in prayer, and the suggestion has often been made that these days are special times of prayer for the unity and mission of the church, but nothing formal has been done about it, as far as I know.

4. The Vigil of Pentecost

The Vigil of Pentecost is not, properly speaking, a vigil—a passing from fast to feast—since it begins in Easter and ends in Easter. It is actually a repetition of the rites of the Easter Vigil for a second baptismal occasion. Unless there are adult catechumens to baptize at Pentecost, or this is the occasion of the bishop's visitation, most parishes will wisely choose to omit the Vigil of Pentecost and baptize infants at the principal Pentecost liturgy. *The Book of Common Prayer* describes the vigil in a single long rubric at the top of page 227.

The altar is vested for Pentecost, with the best red hangings, flowers, and other ornaments. The presider wears a red chasuble or cope and the deacon a red dalmatic and stole. The stand for the paschal candle may be placed near the lectern. The congregation may be given unlighted candles.

The vigil begins with an adaptation of the Service of Light from An Order of Worship in the Evening (BCP 109).

The church is darkened. The procession forms at the back of the nave, led by the deacon carrying the lighted paschal candle. If incense is used, the thurifer may precede the deacon. The presider sings (or says) the Easter acclamation from the church door. The Pentecost *lucernarium* from *The Book of Occasional Services* (BOS 14) may be sung while the altar candles, the candles of the congregation (if they have them), and the lights in the church are lighted, followed by the Prayer for Light for the Easter Season (BCP 111). As noted earlier in section 2.4a on An Order of Worship for the Evening, *The Book of Common Prayer* appears to place the *lucernarium* after the Prayer for Light, but the structure of the *lucernarium*, ending with a versicle and response, suggests that the prayer should follow it. The procession moves through the church to the sanctuary while the *Gloria in excelsis* is sung. The deacon places the paschal candle in its stand. The presider from the chair sings (or says), "The Lord be with you," and the Pentecost collect. At least three readings precede the gospel. Those from which the choice is to be made are:

- Genesis 11:1-9 (the tower of Babel);
- Exodus 19:1-9a, 16-20a; 20:18-20 (the giving of the Law to Moses on Sinai);
- Ezekiel 37:1-14 (the valley of dry bones);
- Joel 2:28-32 (your sons and daughters shall prophesy);
- Acts 2:1-11 (the descent of the Holy Spirit);
- Romans 8:14-17, 22-27 (all who are led by the Spirit of God are children of God).

Presumably the Acts lesson and one of the Old Testament passages will always be included. As at the Great Vigil, it is desirable for a different reader to read each lesson. Each reading is followed by a psalm, canticle, or hymn. The gospel is John 7:37-39a. The deacon reads or sings it in the customary manner. Lights and incense may be used. If there is no deacon, an assisting priest or the presider proclaims the gospel.

The baptisms (or confirmations, if that is the reason for the vigil) take place after the sermon, beginning with the presentation of the candidates. The deacon carries the paschal candle in the procession to the font. The presider may sprinkle the people with the baptismal water while the procession returns to the altar. The preface of Pentecost, the Day of Pentecost seasonal blessing, and the Easter dismissal form a part of the service. For details not repeated here, refer to section 9.4 concerning baptisms at the Great Vigil of Easter.

A reasonable alternative to this vigil is A Vigil on the Eve of Baptism from *The Book of Occasional Services* (BOS 131-135). Baptism is not a part of this vigil, which looks forward to its celebration the next day. The service of light is held as described above, except that the *Phos hilaron*, rather than the *Gloria in excelsis*, is sung. After the Pentecost collect, three lessons, the gospel, and a homily, the candidates and their sponsors come forward. The candidates kneel or bow their heads, and the sponsors each place a hand on the shoulder of their candidate. The priest then lays a hand on the head of each candidate, leads one of two forms of prayer given in *The Book of Occasional Services* (BOS 132-135), a hymn is sung, and the service concludes with a solemn blessing and a dismissal.

Another possible alternative is to use the Vigil of the Resurrection from the Canadian *Book of Alternative Services* provided for Saturday evenings (BAS 133-137). This is an adaptation of an early Christian vigil looking forward to the celebration of the resurrection on the Lord's Day. It also begins with the service of light, but continues with psalms of praise (118 and 150), the resurrection gospel, a Thanksgiving for Water (BAS 135), "The Song of Moses," and a blessing.

5. The Day of Pentecost

Pentecost marks the close of the Great Fifty Days. Its Jewish antecedent celebrated the giving of the Law, and for Christians Pentecost celebrates the outpouring of the Spirit. Although originally the designation of Pentecost as a baptismal feast was intended to encompass the entire fifty days, the Day of Pentecost became a second baptismal feast, often a sort of make-up for those unable to be baptized at Easter. In northern countries it was preferred, because the weather was warmer. The popular English title Whitsunday derives from "white Sunday," so called because the newly baptized were present in the church in their white baptismal robes.

The Prayer Book designates Pentecost as a baptismal feast, and baptisms regularly take place at the principal eucharist on Whitsunday. If there are no baptisms, the Renewal of Baptismal Vows from the Great Vigil replaces the Nicene Creed. It is a major festival and its liturgy should reflect this. This is often difficult in the United States, where it frequently conflicts with Mothers' Day or the Memorial Day weekend. Advance planning is essential.

The color for Pentecost is red, the color of the Holy Spirit. The paschal candle is burning for all services. It is extinguished without ceremony at the conclusion of the last service. The stand for the paschal candle may be moved to the baptistry after the service, so that the candle may be lighted for all baptisms as a symbol of the resurrection.

The liturgy begins with the Easter acclamation, the *Gloria in excelsis* or a proper hymn in its place, and the collect of Pentecost. The *Gloria* is sung immediately after the opening versicles proper to baptism, if they are used, and before "The Lord be with you" (BCP 312). Many parishes take their lead from the question in the Acts lesson, "How is it that we hear, each of us, in our own native language?" and arrange to have the Scripture lessons read in as many different languages as possible. An effective way to do this is to have different readers in succession read Acts 2:1-6 each in a different language, and then one reads (or all read together) the rest of the lesson, beginning with verse 7, in English, or in whatever language the congregation usually worships. Alternatively, or in addition, the gospel may be read in various languages.

The baptisms or renewal of vows follow the gospel and sermon. The Pentecost preface is used, and the Pentecost seasonal blessing may precede the dismissal. The Alleluias are added to the fraction anthem and the dismissal.

Since Pentecost is the final day of Easter, and not the beginning of a new season, the weekdays after Pentecost do not repeat the Sunday propers. The appropriate numbered proper is used throughout the week, and all of the paschal additions to the service are dropped. The paschal cycle has ended for the year, and the church enters the weeks after Pentecost, celebrating the time in which we actually live—the period between the Pentecost and the Second Advent.

Liturgical Resources

Official Publications of the Episcopal Church
The following books are published by the Church Hymnal Corporation,
New York City, New York.
- *The Book of Common Prayer* (1979)
    the Prayer Book of the Episcopal Church; revised in 1979
- *The Book of Occasional Services* (1994)
    *revised every three years to include the actions taken at each
    General Convention*
- *Lesser Feasts and Fasts* (1994)
    *revised every three years to include the actions taken at each
    General Convention*
- *The Altar Book*
    text and rubrics for the eucharistic liturgies of The Book of
    Common Prayer; *includes music for the Exultet and other texts*

- *The Hymnal 1982*
  includes service music and hymns
- *The Hymnal 1982, Accompaniment Edition*
  includes additional service music, harmonies, indicies, etc.
- *Gradual Psalms*
  in seven volumes; contains words and chants for psalms after the first reading, and Alleluias, tracts, and verses in use before the gospel
- *The Passion Gospels* (1992)
  includes plainchant for singing the passion gospels in the New Revised Standard Version; *edited by Ormonde Plater*
- *The Plainsong Psalter* (1988)
  the 150 psalms with antiphons, set to plainchant melodies
- *The Anglican Chant Psalter* (1987)
  the 150 psalms pointed for four-part Anglican chants
- *Supplementary Liturgical Materials* (1996)
  prayers and liturgies in expansive language, approved by General Convention

Official Publication of the Anglican Church of Canada

- *The Book of Alternative Services of the Anglican Church of Canada*. Toronto: Anglican Book Centre, 1985.

Official Publication of the Church of England

- *Lent, Holy Week, Easter: Services and Prayers*. London: Church House Publishing/Cambridge University Press/SPCK, 1986.

Other Liturgical Resources for the Paschal Cycle

- *Casel, Odo. The Mystery of Christian Worship*, ed. Bernard Neunheuser. Westminster, Md.: Newman Press, 1962. (out of print)
- *Celebrating Redemption: The Liturgies of Lent, Holy Week and the Great Fifty Days*. Fort Worth, Tex.: Associated Parishes, 1980.
- Elwood, Frederick C., comp., and John L. Hooker, ed. *In the Shadow of Holy Week: The Office of Tenebrae* (New York: Church Hymnal Corporation, 1996).
- *The Great Vigil of Easter: A Commentary*. Fort Worth, Tex.: Associated Parishes, 1977.
- Galley, Howard E. *The Ceremonies of the Eucharist: A Guide to Celebration*. Cambridge, Mass.: Cowley Publications, 1989.
- Galley, Howard E. *The Prayer Book Office*. New York: Church Hymnal Corporation, 1988.
- Jounel, Pierre. "The Year." In A. G. Martimort, *The Church at Prayer*. Volume IV, *The Liturgy and Time*. Trans. Matthew J. O'Connell. Collegeville: Liturgical Press, 1986.
- Maddux, Earle H., SSJE. *An American Holy Week Manual*. Second Edition. Cambridge, Mass.: Society of Saint John the Evangelist, 1958. (out of print)
- Mitchell, Leonel L. *Planning the Church Year*. Harrisburg: Morehouse Publishing, 1991.
- Mitchell, Leonel L. *Praying Shapes Believing: A Theological Commentary on* The Book of Common Prayer. Harrisburg: Morehouse Publishing, 1985.
- Perham, Michael, and Kenneth Stevenson. *Waiting for the Risen Christ: A Commentary on* Lent, Holy Week, Easter: Services and Prayers. London: SPCK, 1986.
- Plater, Ormonde. *Deacons in the Liturgy*. Harrisburg: Morehouse Publishing, 1992.

- Plater, Ormonde. *Intercession: A Theological and Practical Guide*. Cambridge, Mass.: Cowley Publications, 1995.
- Russell, Joseph P., ed. *The New Prayer Book Guide to Christian Education*. Cambridge, Mass.: Cowley Publications, 1996.
- Shepherd, Massey H., Jr. *Holy Week Offices*. Greenwich: Seabury Press, 1958. (out of print)
- Stevenson, Kenneth. *Jerusalem Revisited: The Liturgical Meaning of Holy Week*. Washington, D.C.: Pastoral Press, 1988.
- Wright, J. Robert. *Readings for the Daily Office from the Early Church*. New York: Church Hymnal Corporation, 1991.

Cowley Publications is a ministry of the Society of St. John the Evangelist, a religious community for men in the Episcopal Church. Emerging from the Society's tradition of prayer, theological reflection, and diversity of mission, the press is centered in the rich heritage of the Anglican Communion.

Cowley Publications seeks to provide books, audio cassettes, and other resources for the ongoing theological exploration and spiritual development of the Episcopal Church and others in the body of Christ. To this end, it is dedicated to developing a new generation of theological writers, encouraging them to produce timely, creative, and stimulating publications of excellence, and making these publications available widely, reaching both clergy and lay persons.